American Foreign Policy

AMERICAN FOREIGN POLICY

AMERICAN
FOREIGN POLICY

BY A DIPLOMATIST

Einstein, Lewis David

BOSTON AND NEW YORK
HOUGHTON MIFFLIN COMPANY
The Riverside Press Cambridge
1909

PREFACE

IT is no unmixed evil that the feeling of confidence in the limitless extent of the country's resources and in its economic self-sufficiency should lately have been shaken. So long as an apparently boundless horizon extended before us, we moved on a plane different from the rest of the world and indifferent thereto. To-day, when for the first time we are beginning to understand that our natural resources are limited, that the end of the nation's possibilities for internal development is almost within sight, and that its capacity of consumption has been unable to keep pace with its production, the necessity of providing foreign markets for our industry is increasingly felt. Accompanying this has come the realization of the need for a navy sufficiently powerful to protect our over-sea

commerce and our coast line, our policies
in Latin America and our distant dependencies in the Pacific. The country has at
last realized the importance of a fleet as
an insurance against war. It has still to
be aroused to the necessity of an efficient
diplomacy as an adjunct to the navy, both
in the extension of our commerce and influence abroad and in the preservation of
peace while carrying out the national policies.

Hitherto our attainment to national greatness has been unaccompanied by the corresponding preparation in the public mind
for a foreign policy conforming to the
magnitude of the country's new responsibilities and the loftiness of its manifest
destiny. American public opinion, only
lately awakened to the importance of intercourse with other nations, has still to be
trained to the consciousness of what it may
rightly demand from diplomacy as an
instrument for the nation's welfare. It
remains weighted by the handicap of tradi-

tions which, though they have outlived their utility, have not yet lost their hold. The same process of renovation which, acting in industry, has borne us into the forefront of nations requires infusion into the mechanism of our foreign policy, in order to adapt it to the present and future exigencies of the Republic's international position.

The purpose of these studies is to draw attention to the duty of diplomacy to further our foreign policy in different regions of the world, and to the conditions of national security upon which must rest its assertion.

THE AUTHOR.

June, 1909.

CONTENTS

AMERICAN FOREIGN POLICY

CHAPTER I

THE POLICY OF UNDERSTANDINGS

OUR prejudice against foreign alliances has been handed down as the tradition of a century, confirmed by the early difficulties the Republic encountered. The result of the Revolution had been to withdraw the new federation from the orbit of European politics. The French fleet sailing from Yorktown cut the cord which linked us with the Old World, and we were left to pursue alone the destinies to which our position and our energies were to summon us. When the acquisition of Louisiana extended the nation's frontiers to the Pacific, our insular position towards Europe offered, save from Canada, no basis for attack, and we were freed from that dread of invasion never absent from the minds of continental statesmen. After the War of 1812, our relations with other countries subsided to a calm level of platonic cordiality, interrupted only by outbursts of sympathy for the cause of liberty abroad, and hardly disturbed except for solicitude with regard to Cuba, Confederate attempts at securing foreign recognition, and, connected therewith, Napoleon the Third's abortive Mexican adventure. The attitude of aloofness we preserved toward the Old World remained practically unchanged for a century. Almost our only point of continuous contact came through the mass of emigrants who were speedily absorbed by the nation's phenomenal growth; and apart from certain Irish efforts to draw us into Anglophobia, the foreign elements in the country have never, in matters of importance, attempted to influence our diplomacy with regard to their lands of origin. The nation was left to effect its internal evolution free from the consideration of problems of foreign policy, and in struggle only with itself.

Where the very existence of a country is at stake, international relations, when they are not immediately threatening, appear of minor consequence. The long struggle leading up to the Civil War and the period of Reconstruction evolving from it had withdrawn our interest from abroad. Occupied by its industrial evolution, the internal development of the country, which required and consumed its remaining energy, pointed to the West. For a century foreign intercourse rightly appeared to the nation to be of secondary importance. In these years when the material foundations of our present position were being laid, the diplomatic experience early difficulties had given us came almost to be forgotten. Economically and politically, the nation's energies were all engaged and absorbed in other directions.

To the outbreak of the Spanish War, we had little or no foreign danger to fear. In

that critical first century of the Republic's
development, the necessity for a national
policy of isolation was manifestly dictated
to our interests. Any other course would
have enmeshed us in the European system
of balances and obviously have hindered
our expansion, even, had it led to no more
baneful result. The wisdom of this policy,
which had impressed itself on the leaders
of both parties, appeared to receive further
consecration from the political testament of
Washington. His counsel had been trans-
mitted from generation to generation, impressive by the weight attached to his great
name. That it was directed not against
alliances, but against entangling alliances,
came almost to be overlooked.

Mr. Olney has justly observed in his
acute analysis [1] of the *Farewell Address*
that, correctly interpreted, it holds as true
to-day as when delivered. Washington
had founded his reasoning on our then
feebleness as a nation and on our remote-

---

[1] *Atlantic Monthly*, May, 1898, pp. 578 *et seq.*

ness in distance and in interest from events of a strictly European order. He had said, to quote again oft-repeated words: —

"Europe has a set of primary interests, which to us have none, or a very remote relation. . . . Our detached and distant situation invites and enables us to pursue a different course. . . . It is our true policy to steer clear of permanent alliances with any portion of the foreign world. . . . Taking care always to keep ourselves, by suitable establishments, on a respectable defensive posture, we may safely trust to temporary alliances for extraordinary emergencies."

Three things ensue from this. While we were to abstain from all participation or interference in the internal affairs of Europe on account of our remote relation thereto, no mention is made of the rest of the world. It may be argued that the future of other continents did not present itself as of importance to Washington's mind. But even if this assumption were true, are we to allow a prescriptive force to govern our attitude toward questions ignored by our first President when he had carefully limited the application of his advice to specific conditions? Secondly, while our remoteness invited a certain line of policy, the need for this once ended, it is presumable that our policy would likewise change in conformity to new requirements. Lastly, he advocated in the clearest unmistakable terms the expediency of temporary alliances for extraordinary emergencies. Indeed, who could have been more sensible to the fact that without a foreign alliance our national independence would hardly have been established?

The marvelous expansion of the country during the last century appears to have amply justified the success of all its policies. But there is an unearned increment even in statecraft. The force of impact of the huge moving mass upon the American continent has perhaps gained more for us than any foresight of statesmanship. In the presence of such diplomatic problems as we have hitherto had to solve, the wisdom or error of a few has been of secondary importance. The country's prosperity has been built on the solid rock of common effort rather than on the individual genius of statesmen. Save perhaps with Lincoln, its destinies have never been intimately tied with those of any single man. This result, while it has firmly established the foundations of the nation's welfare by making them largely independent of governmental action, has not been without drawbacks of another order. Little obvious as these were so long as we remained within an insular wall, they became manifest the day of our emergence from political seclusion.

We had rejoiced in isolation without realizing that the strength we were acquiring was destined to outgrow its limitations, and that almost unconsciously we were laying the foundation upon which the future assertion of our foreign policy was to rest. The accumulation of wealth ap-

peared to be the nation's principal interest.
Politically and economically, the aloofness
which had shielded our infancy, after having been its protection, was beginning to
prove an obstacle to further development.
Yet, paradoxically, we failed to appreciate
the importance of the change which brought
our isolation to an end.

The training of our public life had for a
century been that of domestic politics. The
complications of international relations
with their new responsibilities flashed almost as a revelation before the entire nation,
which found itself on the morrow of the
Spanish War in the presence of problems
as novel as they were unforeseen. Without
realizing either their gravity or their solution, we have since approached these with
calm confidence, a loftiness of purpose characteristic of our highest political ideals.
We have given in Cuba, and are giving now in the Philippines, an example of
national altruism that history has not often
paralleled. The remembrance of our own

past security has caused us, however, to
consider the problems they present less in
their relation to us than in our relation to
them, and to devote correspondingly less
solicitude to the diplomatic and military
exigencies imposed by our dependencies
in order to forestall the possibility of later
humiliation. Our former weakness had
proved our strength. The conquests of
our strength and our fortune have now become our weakness.

By the acquisition of the Philippines we
have assimilated the conditions of our possession to those of other nations holding
Asiatic colonies. Beyond this the occupation of the archipelago affects the assertion of our influence elsewhere, curtailing
the independence of what would otherwise
have been an exclusively American policy
by holding in view the special requirements
of our Asiatic position. From a diplomatic
and military standpoint, the possession of
these dependencies is beyond question such
a source of weakness that it may well be

asked if a public opinion with higher political training would ever have voluntarily
assumed the responsibility of their acquisition, had it been aware of its veritable im-
port. But even a greater weakness, when
considered in the light of similar deficiencies shared by other powers, is far from
being without remedy if we do not voluntarily deprive ourselves thereof.

Emerging from a century's isolation, we
find ourselves at the threshold of a new
era with two roads before us. The one
supposedly traditional in its character counsels us to rely entirely upon our unaided
resources, to be strong in the consciousness of our might as well as of that right
which every nation arrogates as peculiar
to itself. This policy appeals on the surface to the manliness of the nation. Carried to its logical conclusion it might be
practical, but at what sacrifice! A triumph
of militarism would be the only effective
means by which we could assure the safeguarding of our pretensions and over-sea

possessions. Should our ambitions ever clash against those of a state equal to us in sea power, that had adopted the principle of the nation in arms, we could successfully oppose it only at the same cost. Even greater sacrifices would be necessary on our part, since other nations could rely under certain conditions on the aid of allies, from which we should presumably be debarred. In any measure short of an enormous increase in armed strength, so great that no nation or coalition would wish to risk the challenge of our titles, lies danger ahead. A traditional policy inevitably means for us a military policy.

Statesmanship is, above all, guidance in economy of effort. To adjust the requirements of a national policy in conformity with its resources, to see that no greater effort is called for than may be necessary to accomplish a given result, is its method. Armed strength is certainly the foundation of our security, and to neglect it would be to incur greater risk. But while a nation's

safety is purchased only at the price of
constant vigilance and preparation, there
is a limit even to this. Our strength, however great, is only relative — proportionate
neither to the magnitude of our ambitions
nor to the defenselessness of our foreign
policies.

Any undue increase in armaments such
as would be necessary to guarantee us
against all dangers presents two serious
disadvantages. It is costly, especially in a
country without conscription, where military expenditure already meets with mili-
tant opposition. It further conduces to
rivalry on the part of other nations. Moreover, any sudden or unlimited increase
would hardly be in tenor with our repeated
declarations of peaceful intentions. Yet
such is the force of an outworn tradition
that its alternative, or rather its supple-
ment, has hardly been considered. Diplomatic means of defense exist as potent as
military, and the presence of an ally's fleets
may preserve our own from action. The

choice lies before the nation: either we must maintain as many troops in the Philippines as our military advisers judge necessary against all contingencies, and provide as many battleships to guard the oceans which encircle us as our naval advisers deem indispensable, or we must consider the advisability of other measures. Complete isolation from the world's affairs on a nation's part is warranted only by extreme feebleness or confident strength. The fruit of recent victories has now deprived us of former invulnerability. National greatness has not been achieved without the peril of novel responsibilities. We find ourselves exposed to danger both in our South American pretensions and in our Oriental possessions, yet without diplomatic recognition of the first, or allies to aid in protecting the second. It is possible that our strength permits us to dispense with both. But for a peaceful nation we may rely too much on battleships, and not enough on diplomacy.

The most striking development in modern diplomacy has been the vast extension given within quite recent times to the system of arrangements and understandings which now link together the nations of Europe. These differ radically from the eighteenth-century idea of alliances, which were mainly offensive in purpose even when restricted in their liability. The new conception, on the contrary, is eminently pacific in character, and limited in application to comparatively narrow ends. It aims within certain determined regions to preserve actual conditions and to eliminate possible causes of conflict, chiefly in colonial spheres, by taking cognizance of the special or mutual interests of the powers concerned, and lending to the preservation of such agreements the force that is derived by coöperation of effort.

There is reasonable certainty to-day that Europe will never again witness such a coalition as once annihilated Poland. In fact, the dread of spoliation has given rise to this system of mutual insurance. The

European powers, confronted with greater
difficulties than our own, and, perhaps,
possessing more ancient experience in the
handling of foreign affairs, have founded
their security on mutual guarantees intended to preserve policies of common interest. Even Japan, the last comer in the
comity of nations, has in recent years been
too painfully reminded of the absence of
similar precautions not to welcome the
first opportunity of preventing its recur-
rence. For us it may also become advisable
to consider the adoption of a foreign policy
upon a non-partisan basis, upon broader
foundations than would have been warranted by our former position, and in
greater conformity with actual necessities.
We are still somewhat unused to considering questions of this order in their world-
wide aspects. Our situation as a great
nation has been established by the logic of
facts, and without the corresponding intel-
lectual preparation, so impotent when it
does not possess the material foundation

for greatness. Circumstances have placed
us in the forefront of world powers. But
our position has been achieved almost too
easily. We have not experienced the dis-
cipline of adversity which has schooled
other great states. We have not felt the
need for caution in our acts of international
significance. We have gone ahead almost
without a policy other than the Monroe
Doctrine and our traditional non-entan-
glement. At the present juncture, even
though the benefits of our new importance
are mainly apparent, and we rightly look
forward with confident hope to the future,
it may be advisable for a prudent statecraft to take cognizance of the possibility of
shoals in the course that lies before us. Our
diplomacy ought to concern itself with the
preparation of a policy which will enable
us, so far as human foresight can foretell,
to escape such perils while pursuing our
destiny as a great nation.

The past has brought us into contact
with the Old World both in its collective

form as an aggregate of states and with the individual European powers. In the formulation of any policy the experience of history cannot be disregarded, and we have to bear in mind the nature of the danger which may beset us. The continental nations have always inclined, when their contemplated action lay outside Europe, to collective manifestations, as being of a nature to diminish their risk and increase their force, while protecting them from danger behind. We have witnessed the effects of such concerted action against Japan, robbed at Port Arthur of the prize of victory over China. We have seen it operating with varying success against Turkey. We have heard its rumblings, however faint, even against ourselves. The very admission that this peril may conceivably exist means that we cannot with impunity disinterest ourselves from European politics. The future possibility of a concert of powers can never leave us indifferent. More than ever our new dependencies make us vulnerable and offer pawns for possible enemies to take from us.

American diplomacy can have no more important mission than that of guarding against this danger, which would be brought about by the hegemony of one state over others in banding them together for a common purpose. The first principles of our policy demand that we view with disfavor the efforts of any power to assert its own predominant superiority over weaker neighbors. A coalition becomes dangerous when it is guided by a single power. When nations enter upon a strictly equal footing their efforts are too often at variance to be easily effective. American diplomacy has a definite scope before it in exercising watchfulness against the occurrence of such a peril. Nor is our solicitude exclusively political. We should remember what a European commercial union, advocated by many foreign statesmen and economists, would mean for us. Even if such union were without apparent or immediate po-

litical scope, its formation, directed mainly
against our trade, would create for America
a most serious peril: German customs unity
preceded German political unity.

Yet neither hostile alliance nor coalition
need alarm us so long as we do not voluntarily cripple ourselves by ignoring the
means at our command to resist these.
This does not imply the necessity for action
on our part in events of a strictly European
order. The disappearance of Dutch independence, if so unfortunate an event were
ever to take place, would, for instance, be
keenly regretted by us, but, except for the
fate of Holland's colonies, it would not
warrant our intervention. Still less would
any concern we might feel in the ultimate
disposition of Austria be likely to justify
military action on our part. The diplomatic solicitude we have in Europe is and
should remain that of spectators. But our
interests are now too widely spread to
permit us longer to disinterest ourselves
from any concerted action of the powers,

with its almost inevitable extra-European ramifications.

It is only a short step for European influence to extend beyond the Continent and enter into spheres which concern us as well. The line to draw is indeed far more subtle than may at first appear. History bears witness that in diplomacy unimportant beginnings have often unexpected consequences. It is to guard against unpleasant surprises of this nature that we should neglect no opportunity in identifying our action with that of the European states. The more we assert the equality of our rights and responsibilities with theirs, the more we make felt our legitimate influence in the councils of nations, the less likelihood will there be of the formation of any coalition, commercial or political, in opposition to our interests. Political movements possess in themselves an organic growth, and such future danger as may exist for us could more easily acquire head by our aloofness at the time of its inception than by our opposition thereto. Its maturity would present for us greater peril than its infancy. Nor if we act prudently need we ever feel ourselves alone in resisting it. Europe, even under its present cover of friendliness toward us, contains many conflicting interests, and certain of these would normally be favorable to our policy.

We can hardly suppose, however, that the extension unavoidably taken by our diplomacy will not encounter resistance. No power can hope to be successful without incurring the antagonism of others, even though our own peaceful proclivities should preclude us from the former rapacious ambitions of Old World states. But whatever future struggles await us, we cannot forget that diplomacy, like war, may achieve for us victories or defeats. However powerful we may become, a combination may array against us power as great. The burden of our weight, on whichever side of the scales we incline, will inevitably be counterpoised. Even more it will lead almost inevitably to fresh distributions of strength. While the present grouping of triple "entente" and triple alliance, each reënforced by subsidiary aids, may not prove everlasting, it is likely to provide the basis upon which such new accretions will form. Yet even future combinations need not concern us. The balancing of strength is no menace of war. On the contrary, the distribution of liability in such an event among several nations is the most certain guarantee of peace.

Bellicose tendencies are far more likely to exist in a single nation than where several are allied together, and modern alliances tend either to act in the direction of peace, or else to limit the scene of conflict. The recent Russo-Japanese War affords the best example of how the efforts of Great Britain and France, in spite of their respective alliances to each of the contestants, succeeded in isolating the field of hostilities.

As for the argument that our present strength is sufficient, examples are not wanting of states with fleets and armies greater than our own who feel that the interests of peace would best be preserved by a policy of understandings. England, with a sea force far superior to ours, has looked to diplomacy to aid her navy in guarding the British Empire. Allied with Japan, another understanding links her with France, while in the event of war her fleets can make use of Portugal's unrivaled strategic position in the South Atlantic in return for guaranteeing the latter's colonial possessions. Diplomacy has been used by England as an adjunct to naval strength, and her policy has neglected no step to further secure the safeguard of India as the pivot of the British Empire. By these alliances, culminating in the recent agreement with Russia, she has guarded every avenue of approach to her great colony. It may be urged that England's exposed position necessitates such precautions. But has she any possession more vulnerable than are the Philippines?

The colonial position of France more
closely resembles our own. With dependencies situated at great distance from the
home country, she had felt herself unable
to protect these in the event of certain contingencies. In spite of the lengthy period
of Anglophobia occasioned by colonial rivalry through which she had passed, her
diplomacy effected an understanding with
Great Britain. France by this means obtained a protection for her dependencies
greater than her fleet could give. To this
she has added a further guarantee. The
defenselessness of Indo-China and the feeling that it lay at the mercy of Japan had
been the first lesson of the late war to impress her. Without slighting the susceptibilities of her Russian ally, France has been
able to negotiate an agreement with Japan
guaranteeing each other's possessions in the
Far East.

After these examples of nations possessing colonies, yet supplementing their
powers of defense by the aid of other states,

we may consider the conditions in which a similar understanding would be advisable for the United States. The problem presents itself of finding a desirable partner willing to enter into a well-defined mutual insurance, with whom no conflicting interests are likely to clash. Our old prejudice against alliances had Europe in view, and to-day, as in the past, any treaty or pact which would entangle us in the internal affairs of the Old World would be condemned. But it is difficult to see the inexpediency of an arrangement which, without adding a ship to our fleet, or a dollar to our expenditure, would restrict the nation's liability to the American continent and the islands of the Pacific, in return for guaranteeing the *status quo* from Maine to Manila; which would effectively protect the Monroe Doctrine and the Panama Canal, and safeguard the integrity of our dependencies, and in removing the Pacific from the sphere of political change would assure us the sovereignty of the

Philippines for such eventual disposition as the American people deem fit to make. Can it be doubted that an understanding of this nature would immeasurably strengthen our position and our policies, and be a further guarantee for the preservation of peace?

The price to pay for these benefits would be too heavy if we should be dragged as the result into a continental conflagration, and obliged to take sides in a struggle between the nations of Europe. But the consequence of our understanding with either of the interested parties, in the event of its being engaged in a European conflict, would almost certainly be to restrict and limit the seat of hostilities by removing the American continent, and such parts of the Pacific as might be included within its scope, from the field of operations. The alternative is obvious. If any hostile power chose to disregard our warning and challenge our ally within the bounds which we had declared should be removed from the

scene of conflict, the clearest dictates of
self-preservation would impel us to take
arms for a cause which would then become
our own. But this contingency is almost
too improbable to mention.

Such an understanding would thus be
of an essentially peaceful nature, tending
only to preserve existing conditions by removing all motive for their disturbance.
In contracting it, we should be entering into
a mutual insurance limited by the terms of
the agreement, which would conceivably
restrict its provisions to the guarantee of
actual conditions within the lines of lon-
gitude embracing the American continent
and the Pacific. Providing, therefore, the
nation or nations with which such understanding had been entered into were sufficiently powerful, we need feel no concern
for the future of the Philippines, the safety
of the Panama Canal, or the continuance
of the Monroe Doctrine. And while respect for the latter may be obtained by
different means, the security of our Asiatic

possessions can hardly be assured by any other feasible method.

As an American power and as an Asiatic power, we have to deal with other American and Asiatic powers, considering these in the light of possible friends or adversaries with the consequences attached to each contingency. It is the province of statesmanship to sort the threads of our interests and to see wherein these lie parallel with theirs, and, where they may be dissimilar, to endeavor in times of national calm to adjust causes of friction. The practical advantages of such a process of diplomatic housecleaning have been witnessed in the recent agreements effected by Great Britain with France and Russia. Their differences have now been reconciled. Their diplomatic work has been a labor of peace, and the danger of war, which for so long appeared imminent, has been removed. Diplomacy has given the lie to the "inevitable conflict" so long foreshadowed between these states, and spared each nation concerned its treasure and its blood, making of former enemies present friends.

We have a far easier task. Yet although no such differences or ambitions divide us from other powers, causes of friction lie not far away. But partly out of respect for a tradition that has survived its utility, partly because of still other reasons, we have not availed ourselves of the diplomatic advantages at hand in fortifying our position. We have not utilized the power of diplomacy and made of it a veritable instrument to strengthen national policies. It still lies before us as a peaceful means to forestall the danger of war and remove the causes of national concern.

CHAPTER II

RELATIONS WITH EUROPE

WE had so long been regarded as a peaceful republic, occupied solely by trade, that Europe was startled by our victory over Spain to realize that we possessed ambitions similar to those which for centuries had spurred on her peoples to assert their influence beyond the seas. It is only half correct, however, to say that the war caused our advent as a world power. It inaugurated a new period less than it hastened the development of a growing movement in American national evolution which by its means attained to earlier maturity, but which must in any event have sooner or later made itself felt.

Certain causes would inevitably have terminated our period of former isolation. The extension given to our commercial interests abroad had already for some time aroused keener interest in the world's affairs. So long as American export trade formed but a relatively small proportion of the country's industrial production we were economically independent in our seclusion. When foreign commerce, however, assumed an importance which has lately amounted to over three thousand million dollars annually, any curtailment in its volume meant serious injury to our industry. Yet the closer interest we now feel in the world's affairs has been brought about, not so much by the desire to enlarge our trade and the pressure of material stakes as by the higher consciousness of new responsibilities.

Whereas formerly we accepted without compunction, in questions of international interest, the benefits of other powers' exertions without ourselves incurring corresponding liabilities, the nation's sense of dignity has at last been awakened to this impropriety, and can never again relapse in such matters to its former callousness. The relief of the legations at Pekin has demonstrated our readiness to participate in affairs of joint concern to civilized states.

Except for Great Britain, the result of the Spanish War had been little welcome to the rest of Europe, grown accustomed to the thought that the destinies of the universe should forever be in the hands of five or six of its states. The nations of Europe have been aptly compared by M. d'Haussonville to a party of gamblers seated around a green cloth grown somewhat shabby with age, where each in turn takes the bank. A newcomer enters, his pockets bulging with gold, and startles the players into a fear that he may at once break the bank.

In destroying the time-worn conception as to the exclusive supremacy of Europe we appeared as intruders, and as such were unwelcome. But this resentment has partly disappeared since the more recent victory of Japan made the Old World recover from its first surprise. The Continent recognized that our appearance might offer com-

pensations in neutralizing the new power of
the East, and viewed our recent Japanese
difficulties with thinly veiled satisfaction.
Our single entry as a great nation had for
a time overturned all former calculations
and shifted the axis of power. But offset
by Japan, the scales are only more heavily
weighted than before, and the fulcrum has
been set back where it was, though the
balance is less delicately adjusted. Change
has come through the enlargement of what
had been a restricted horizon to its present
globe-embracing proportions. A concert
of world powers has dispossessed the concert of Europe.

While the European nations are rapidly
adapting their diplomacy to conform with
the new requirements, we have emerged
from our former aloofness handicapped by
the weight of a traditional policy no longer
in touch with actual conditions. Brought
up to respect the wisdom of non-entangle-
ment in the affairs of Europe, we now find
ourselves called upon to assume our place

as a world power, yet unable to separate
the international position of foreign states
from their strictly European position, or to
forget that the general interests of civilized
nations are likewise in great measure the
interests of Europe. Our attitude toward
such countries must be related to our colonial situation, and it may even vary according as their over-sea policy affects our own.
Foreign relations have grown for us in com-
plexity, and our requirements have ceased
to bear the same uniform hall-mark of
simplicity in every region of the globe. We
must scan more critically the movements
and the ambitions of other states, without
being able as before to disinterest ourselves
therefrom. The vital interests of each of
the great European powers concern us in
relation to our policy.

To begin with a sister republic, tradition
and sympathy cause us to regard France
as the most ancient of our friends, to whom
we have been bound by a debt of gratitude
not yet forgotten. Our friendship toward

her rests on a solid basis, nor are conflicting
ambitions likely again to clash between us.
As an American power, France's possessions, of slight consequence and far scattered from the St. Lawrence to Guiana,
are mainly of historical importance; but as
Asiatic powers, the interests of the two
republics are similar.   Even economically
there is little reason to anticipate between
the two nations that acute commercial
rivalry which so often precedes political
difficulties.   The active participation of
France in the world's affairs is now confined to a rôle of peace.   There is slight
probability of her ever again seeking to pursue the course of aggression that so often
made her in the past the disturbing factor
in Europe. With reason, therefore, may we
look to the future continuance of our ancient friendship.

From having been the most warlike,
France has in recent years become the most
peaceful of states. Her former policies of
adventure have been definitely dismissed,

and like another and greater Holland she
has subsided into a rich capitalist nation,
farming out her millions for others more
active to employ profitably. Since the war
of 1870 her colonial policy has been dictated less by need for expansion than
through fear on the part of her statesmen
lest their country be outdistanced in the
future, if new national interests were not
created beyond the seas. Successful in
this field, her colonial enterprise, save in
North Africa, is no longer aggressive.

France has ceased to be a menace to any
state. But her continental position imposes upon her a certain policy. Lying
between two powerful neighbors, the choice
had become necessary between accepting the consequences of naval inferiority
toward Great Britain and military inferiority toward Germany. Friendship with the
one power meant a guarantee for her colonial empire in the event of war, but at the
risk of invasion; friendship with the other
meant inviolability of territory, but the al-

most certain loss of colonies in case of such
a contest.

Her feeling of resentment toward Germany had been greatly lessened in recent
years. The sting of bitterness caused by
the remembrance of lost provinces, if not
forgotten, was at least relegated to the rear
by the more recent smart of national humiliation suffered at Fashoda. Counsels were
therefore divided as to what policy to adopt,
when the events which led to the Moroccan Conference demonstrated that France
could secure the Emperor's friendship only
by unreservedly accepting German hegemony. And however great the anxiety to
insure the safety of her eastern frontier,
French patriotism revolted at accepting a
situation which would have forced the
nation to acquiesce in the position of
an inferior power definitely submissive to
German policy. Hence the understanding
with England, at first of strictly colonial
interest, afterward assumed a new and unexpected importance, the significance of

which recent developments have further augmented.

While France to-day seeks only to preserve her present possessions, Germany is too lately born among great nations to have enjoyed the inheritance of older states. Hitherto her efforts to colonize have not been altogether successful, and her foreign dependencies remain far inferior to those of even small powers like Holland or Portugal. With a rapidly growing population ill confined within the present frontiers, and confronted by grave social problems, she aims to follow the example of her neighbors in securing outlets for over-sea trade and enterprise. But while other great powers have reached a stage where they are content to develop what is theirs, Germany feels that she has not yet reached her full measure, nor has her national energy attained its zenith. She seeks a position where she will be able to demand participation in, or compensation for, any alteration or change in existing territorial conditions, in whatever quarter of the globe it occurs; and to prepare for this the same careful labor is to-day going on in the German navy as took place in the Prussian army after the defeat of Jena. Will a united Germany care to wait fifty years to witness results? Success engenders the wish for success, and the remembrance of past victories has been too vivid not to spur on future hope.

Such ambitions as Germany may cherish are accompanied by armaments of a nature which not unnaturally cause solicitude among neighbors at whose expense they would be carried out. However unfair it would be to criticise her for an efficiency which her neighbors may envy, which has proved the reason for her past success, and the burden of which concerns her alone, it would be unwise to fail to appreciate its consequences. Her deficiency in sea power alone prevents her from wielding the same world power which she enjoys as a continental state, and to remedy this Germany's present efforts are strained. Her imme-

diate goal is not the acquisition of a paramount naval position, which she knows
herself unable under existing conditions to
wrest from Great Britain, but the bringing
about of a state of armed peace on sea, as
on land, which would terminate the latter's
supremacy. The policy of armed peace
has made Germany the dominant force on
the Continent since 1870, and her successful pursuit of a similar condition on the
high seas would no longer render hopeless
a possible naval contest with Great Britain.
German naval policy to-day aims so to
enlarge her present fleet as to make it, even
single-handed, a dangerous adversary, while
it would always constitute the nucleus of
a possible array of forces which might be
marshaled against a common foe. The conception is Napoleonic in spirit. Napoleon
aimed to place himself at the head of a
European confederation definitely submissive to his policy; and German influence is
to-day dominant not only in Austria, her
avowed ally, but in several of the smaller

states of northern and eastern Europe.
But her political allies, while strong in their
military armaments, are crippled by an in-
adequacy of sea power which would render
their assistance of slight utility in the event
of naval war. In order to fulfill her ambition, Germany requires both to isolate her
rival and to obtain the aid of a power able
to prove of assistance to her on the sea. At
the present time we are the nation best fitted
to render her such services. Our resources
and our naval strength would be of inesti-
mable advantage to the emperor in a possible war with England, and the cultivation
of our friendship may well appear a desirable goal toward which his diplomacy should
strive.

The former vapors of conflict between
Germany and ourselves are fortunately
long since dissipated. Her supposed coveting of the Philippines after the battle of
Manila was keenly resented by us. But the
details of this episode would prove that her
conduct, to which we then took exception,

had been due to indiscretions for which she
was in no way to blame. Her subsequent
course has certainly been altogether loyal,
and we have even had occasion to appreciate in regions of special interest to us the
friendliness of her present diplomacy. All
recollection of unpleasantness is happily
effaced, and German official relations have
more than oscillated to the extreme pole of
friendship. This is eminently desirable,
and so long as it does not cause us to forget
vital interests, we can but gain by the preservation of the present fortunate cordiality.
We cannot blind ourselves, however, to the
fact that Germany desires our amity, inspired by deeper motives than may appear
on the surface. Even if our active aid could
not be enlisted, to endeavor to detach us
from other sympathies is legitimate diplomacy on her part. From our standpoint,
however, the benefits of any closer intimacy
than at present exists would be hardly com-
mensurate with the corresponding disadvantages suffered in other quarters. The

present cultivation of friendship with so great a power, and from whom we have much to learn, is to be earnestly desired, but any closer understanding with Germany would present for us too many obstacles to be enduring or advantageous.

The preponderant influence of Germany in European affairs has been somewhat heightened by the temporary exclusion of Russia from her accustomed place in the councils of nations and her condemnation for the next few years to a rigid policy of internal development. The period of Muscovite aggression is over, for a time at least, and as a constitutional state she has settled with good grace to the acceptance of a new rôle of peace. Her recent understanding with Great Britain, which brought to an end long-standing jealousies, was welcome to us. We had no cause to desire the perpetuation of disputes between powers whose interests so closely resemble our own. In the past, amity with Russia has been a wise tradition in our diplomacy, and its continuance should prove an important factor in our future European policy. The causes of friction that have lately arisen over questions of jurisdiction in Manchuria are of passing significance. It is unlikely that divergent interests of vital consequence will ever separate the two nations, while circumstances are easily conceivable, in the extreme Orient, in which they could render each other mutual services.

In addition to political considerations, our commercial interests cause us to desire a closer intimacy with Russia, whose Asiatic expansion, with its consequent needs, is not unlike our own winning of the West. In the struggle for the trade of the Near and Far East, and even in the development of European Russia, numerous opportunities are likely to occur where Russian influence, unable itself to profit, would incline to favor our enterprise in preference to that of other nations.

With the remaining continental powers, apart from the extensive commercial relations we have with them, the protection and development of which necessitate a more watchful diplomacy than is commonly supposed, our interest arises largely from their affiliations with Germany, or with the Dual Alliance, and Great Britain. While Austrian diplomacy has in recent years been increasingly subordinated to that of Berlin, Italian has steered a more independent course. The expression of fidelity to allies and loyalty to friends, so frequently invoked by succeeding Italian Ministers of Foreign Affairs in explanation of their country's foreign policy, likewise characterizes its nature. The course of conciliatory opportunism in harmony with the country's welfare predicates for Italy a cordiality toward both sides which would tend to make for her neutrality in the event of war. This augurs well for the continuance of the many sympathies which unite us to Italy, whose ambitions are unlikely to forebode for us any unexpected or unwelcome developments.

At the present time, when every year

witnesses a growth in the friendship existing between Great Britain and ourselves,
it may appear fanciful to speak of the possibility of conflict between two kindred nations. But the recollection of a Venezuelan
boundary dispute is not long enough removed to allow us to forget what might
have occurred without Lord Salisbury's wise
statesmanship. The efforts of the two governments to smooth all sources of trouble
at a time like the present, when both nations
are animated by the friendliest feelings, is a
wise indication of the importance attached
to such amity.

Towards England the clearest dictates
of reason impel us to turn,— not because of
the intimate ties of language, blood, and civilization, nor because the two nations have
shared a common past. Bonds of sympathy
and kinship have never prevented fratrici-
dal strife; where conflicting interests oppose
they offer a poor foundation upon which to
base an understanding. Identical interests
undivided by divergent ambitions afford

a far safer basis for friendship between nations.

The most serious foreign danger which has menaced us in the past as a nation was the triumph of Napoleon over continental Europe. As Mr. Olney has remarked,[1] were his career ever again to approach or even to threaten repetition, not merely sentiment and sympathy, but the strongest consideration of self-preservation and self-defense, might drive us to take sides. Had the power of England then been annihilated, it is unlikely that we would have attained our present greatness. Great Britain, though fighting us at sea, yet saved us from greater peril. Danger for her, just as danger for us, lies in a coalition of powers, and, in consequence, British diplomacy has to oppose the combinations of Europe. For the past three centuries England's continuous policy has been to resist the efforts of any state to achieve a European hegemony or to assert a paramount influence. When

[1] *Atlantic Monthly*, March, 1900, p. 298.

Spain was dominant she opposed her. A century later she fought Louis the Fourteenth, and alone she faced Napoleon, and later resisted Russia. Time and time again she has manifested her readiness to block any concert of powers directed toward an end distasteful to her. Canning barring the action of the Holy Alliance on the morrow of the Congress of Verona; Palmerston refusing to unite with Napoleon the Third, eager to destroy our unity by aiding the South; Salisbury prepared to thwart any European coalition at the outbreak of the Spanish War, are so many illustrations in point. The aid England was ready to extend us during our recent war proved unnecessary, since no hostile coalition attained maturity. But the fact that, had it been otherwise, the dictates of self-preservation would have compelled our acceptance thereof, just as we accepted the aid of France in the Revolution, gives the lie to the reverence with which we still regard a misinterpreted tradition. Alliances can be entangling only when they are disadvantageous. To guard against their being so is the duty of a wise statesmanship.

Without regarding any power as hostile, we cannot avoid the conclusion that only from England, from the Continent, or from Japan could serious danger menace us. While England as the mistress of the sea would be our most formidable adversary, she could also be our most useful friend, and her friendship is of as much importance to us as is ours to her. Mutual benefit or mutual injury would alike be greater than either could experience at the hands of other nations. While no incentive for hostility exists on either side, with no other power would the advantages of an understanding be so great or the liabilities so small. England controls the key of the situation for us both toward the Continent and toward Japan. Under existing circumstances, were she unwilling, no power could menace us. Nor are such circumstances likely to alter so long as the Continent remains divided.

To guard against this is the primary object
of British diplomacy, and her present guarantee against a united Europe lies in the
understanding with France. What France
is to England, England is to us. Hence the
preservation of the Anglo-French understanding, and in smaller degree the understanding with Russia, concern us only a
little less than the main participants. So
long as these subsist the British navy is supreme, and with our own maintained at such
strength as to make us a formidable factor
in the event of complications, we need fear
no hostile coalition to menace our policies
or our dependencies. Looking toward the
Far East, Mr. Olney has reminded us that
except for Great Britain's countenance we
should almost certainly never have secured
the Philippines.[1] Her alliance with Japan,
coupled with the consciousness of her naval
supremacy, holds that power in restraint;
while in China our policies are united in
upholding the open-door principle. In every

[1] *Atlantic Monthly*, March, 1900, p. 300.

region of the globe we find similarity in
our political interests. And the reason is
unquestionably because England, with the
greatest colonial empire the world has yet
witnessed, can seek only to preserve her
birthright and not to expand further. Land-
glutted, she desires to retain her present
possessions without coveting the territories
of others.

The maintenance of that empire excites
no jealousy in us, and presents no inconvenience. The Philippine experiment has
allayed whatever lurking ambitions existed
within us in the direction of colonial expansion beyond the western hemisphere.
While for better or for worse the nation's
destinies must for an indefinite time be
connected with our Oriental dependencies,
we have no desire to enlarge such experience. On the contrary, we should prefer to
see the colonial markets of the world con-
trolled by a state ready to throw them open
to all comers.

The problems of imperial responsibility

for the acts of self-governing British colonies still remain to be solved; but their intention to exclude the yellow races brings these close to a policy which must henceforth be our own. In that as well lies the opportunity for future coöperation of mutual advantage. Lastly, we cannot forget that Canada is too integral a part of the American continent for its welfare not to be connected with our own. While this is not the place to enter into the problems, more intricate than vital, that still remain to be settled with our northern neighbor, it is obvious that the closer the ties binding us to the mother country, the easier will be their solution. Questions like those of the Newfoundland fisheries can never assume a violent form if the colonists realize that overt acts on their part will deprive them of their government's support.

The furtherance of such a policy of close intimacy with Great Britain necessitates a frank exchange of views on all matters of common interest. But such understanding

would have little in common with the nature
of an alliance. It would base itself rather
on the desire to settle outstanding questions which have in the past been causes
of friction, and further to unite in the mutual declaration of a policy of joint interest
which would tend to perpetuate existing
conditions, particularly in the Pacific, where
our desires are identical. The fact that our
policies would cause us to regard with disfavor the effort of any nation to disturb
present conditions within spheres of common interest, does not imply that we should
be drawn thereby into conflicts alien to us.
Contact even with the Old World is not
synonymous with entanglement, nor does
entanglement of necessity mean war. England, which has continually mingled in continental affairs, has yet since Waterloo gone
through but one European war. Her efforts
in the direction of her traditional policy are
indeed more likely to be peacefully effective
if our own approval thereof be well understood. The influence of the two great naval

powers, already united by so many intimate
ties, directed toward this end would more
than in any other way strengthen the cause
of peace.

A guarantee on the part of the two countries to maintain the present territorial and
political conditions within certain determined regions could hardly be viewed as
an entangling alliance. It would rather be
a pledge against war, since it would permit
us to dispense with the unlimited extension
of armaments otherwise necessary to defend
our policies, while freeing England from
anxiety with regard to her American colonies and uniting both nations in guaranteeing the integrity of weaker neutral states.
It would offer a permanent basis for our
foreign policy worthy of our dignity as a
great power. And if later, as a result of this,
additional agreements and understandings
tending to the preservation of certain desired conditions within definite spheres
were to be contracted with other states similarly interested, these could hardly be re-

garded as entangling us in the labyrinth of European politics, or otherwise than as bespeaking our sincere desire for peace and our determination to assist its preservation by diplomatic as well as by military means.

CHAPTER III

THE RECOGNITION OF THE MONROE DOCTRINE

THE external problems hitherto confronting the nation have been mainly of a simple order. Since the birth of the Republic we have been spared the intricate questions of foreign policy that disturb the calm of European statesmen. Our diplomacy, after the remarkable success of its early efforts, brought to the consideration of international relations a directness of vision and of method, differing, perhaps, from that of a trained service, but not unsuited to accomplish its end. With neither the glamour nor the brilliancy occasionally present among European diplomatists, our public men have for the most part treated foreign relations with the sterling sense and integrity of purpose characteristic of the best traditions in our government.

So long as national conditions remained

unaltered there was little necessity for change in method. Isolation afforded the best guarantee for our security, and the ocean provided an effectual barrier for possible diplomatic shortcomings. The Spanish War, with the responsibilities it created, sharply marks the inauguration of a new era in the country's development, the importance of which history will only accentuate. But nowhere have its effects been more marked and less realized than in our diplomatic position. We have readily appreciated the difference made in our status from a colonial, military, naval, even from a constitutional standpoint. To a less degree have we been conscious of the change caused in our international relations.

It is a common though hardly an accurate remark that the Spanish War awakened Europe to a sense of our greatness as a nation. Though this was true of the masses on the Continent, there were many public men abroad fully aware of our resources and our capabilities. It was rather that the

Old World, having grown accustomed to consider us as a colossus self-contained, and voluntarily abstaining from all external interference, suddenly realized, as we ourselves with no less surprise realized, that that day was over and that henceforth we were ready to assume our part in the world.

With justifiably ambitious views of the future to which we believe our destinies direct us, we have not yet renovated, so to speak, the mechanism of our action. Certain of our methods still remain unadapted to new conditions, unchanged from what they were at a time when the country's responsibilities were slight and its foreign problems simple. We still view international relations with the same directness of vision as before, without fully appreciating the possibilities which lie before us or the methods which a more difficult position would urge us to employ. The nation at large is hardly conscious that we have to-day outgrown an antiquated system which under actual conditions is hardly conducive to our security.

Other measures have become necessary in order to safeguard the foreign relations of a great state that has to defend over-sea dependencies and a policy which is one of the greatest burdens ever voluntarily assumed by any nation.

Although the Monroe Doctrine has passed into an article of national creed which, irrespective of party, appears almost axiomatically to embody our foreign policy, the reverence with which it inspires us does not equally impress other nations. It would be doing the country poor service to lull it into believing that the European powers accept the doctrine in the same spirit as ourselves, or that its present maintenance reposes on any other ultimate basis than that of force. In the past we have tacitly endeavored to secure its recognition by abstaining from all assertion of our authority abroad. We treated Europe as a monarchical entity and expected similar consideration for republican institutions in America. But we lost sight of the fact that when this policy was inaugurated we were in no position to warrant the great European powers entering into such a bargain. Few things come gratuitously, particularly in diplomacy. When in later years, although able to make our voice heard, we offered no direct compensation in return for favors we did not ask, other nations felt under no obligation to bind themselves to the acceptance of our view.

The acquisition of the Philippines, resulting in the extension of American power into Asiatic waters, deprived us, in the mind of Europe, of whatever moral justification we might previously have possessed for the Monroe Doctrine. According to the idea that had been prevalent abroad, the sole basis for our right in venturing to exclude the Old World from regarding the New as a field for further colonial aggrandizement lay in restricting our activities to the western hemisphere. The fact that such had been our course since the birth of the Republic appeared to give additional sanction to this

idea. When, therefore, the Philippines became an American possession, we seemed
in the eyes of Europe to have forfeited all
moral claim to our contention. This loss,
however, was more than counterbalanced
in other directions. The acquisition of new
dependencies and the vast growth of American influence in every quarter of the globe
gave us a prestige far more diplomatically
negotiable than the position we had left behind. That we have fully availed ourselves
of the new benefits obtained is, however,
questionable. Antiquated traditions have
caused us to neglect the diplomatic means
wherewith to strengthen our position and
effect a security for our policies far greater
than any moral right could ever confer.

The nation, peace-loving, yet determined
at all costs to uphold the Monroe Doctrine,
has not devoted its attention toward the
pacific methods of bringing this about. We
have omitted to do in its support what
powers like France and England, in the face
of far stronger opposition than any encoun-

tered by us, have accomplished in countries
where their action was less justifiable than
our own, but where they have acquired for
their position a sanction which the acquiescence of the only powers able to dispute
their titles has legitimized. England, for
instance, having first obtained the recognition of her occupation of Egypt from the
non-interested powers, secured it finally by
diplomatic means from France, in spite of
the latter's previous animosity, which on
more than one occasion had brought the two
nations to the verge of war. Similarly in her
seizure of Tunis, France first obtaining the
aid of Germany, eager at that time to divert
her former enemy to colonial enterprises,
and later winning over British support, her
position became legalized in the face of the
hostility of Italy, who felt unable to dispute it single-handed and was finally forced
to content herself with the recognition of
shadowy eventual claims over Tripoli.

We have been unaccustomed to consider
this order of negotiation, and have not been

aroused by lack of success to the necessity of taking diplomatic precautions. Under past conditions, the simplicity of our former methods and requirements was sufficient to permit us to dispense therewith. But now that our liabilities have more than kept pace with enlarged resources we cannot afford to forget the hostility which the "brazenly impudent" Monroe Doctrine, as Bismarck once termed it, has encountered abroad, or the frank denunciation it has met on the part of public men and political writers on the Continent. Although this animosity is temporarily quiescent, our diplomacy has still abundant scope before it in endeavoring to counteract such a prejudice.

But for the Philippines we might have been indifferent to the dislike of Europe. To the weakness caused by our pretensions in South America we have added the weakness caused by Asiatic acquisitions. If ever the Monroe Doctrine is challenged, its fate may well be disputed in the waters of Manila Bay. There exists, however, an essential dif-

ference in the degree of exposure between
our position in the Philippines and our
assertion of the Monroe Doctrine. While
without a policy of understandings the security of the former can hardly be assured,
the latter may be safeguarded by obtaining
its recognition from the only powers able
to challenge it. By peaceful methods, as
effectively as by a more aggressive policy,
we are able to guarantee its preservation.
No nation will to-day break solemn obligations without considerable incentive or provocation. If ever the recognition of the great
European powers is, therefore, accorded to
a policy which menaces no peace-loving
state, the dangers of war in questions rising
out of the interpretation of the Monroe
Doctrine will be reduced to insignificance.
Where England and France have obtained
the acquiescence of other powers for colonial ventures of questionable character,
we can secure similar recognition for our
policy. To certain nations of Europe its
acceptance would be a matter of indif-

ference; to one it would undoubtedly be welcome.

Great Britain has often given us the proof of her sincere friendship. An English statesman first suggested the Monroe Doctrine, and the strength of England in the days of our weakness made possible its preservation. Great Britain, with a still dominant trade in South America, is almost as interested as ourselves that no portion of that continent should be alienated to the advantage of any European power. French interests are similar to those of England. Apart from the natural desire to round out the boundaries of her great African empire, France has to-day no other colonial ambition than to preserve what is already hers, least of all one of the serious nature which the challenge of our policy would require. And although the doctrine has in itself been an object of dislike to certain French political writers, the influence of their ideas, which tended in another sphere toward alliance with Germany and a European con-

federation, has greatly diminished in recent
years.

In Russia, as well, we have often found
a friend who would be the more ready to
recognize our contention in South America,
as she is herself without ambitions or interests in the western hemisphere.

Only two European powers are conceivably likely at any time to challenge the
Monroe Doctrine, and one of these could
not be in a position to do so for many years.
Germany and Italy are alike in possessing
great interests in South America. The danger of interference by the former in southern Brazil has been frequently commented
upon, and although the present cordial relations existing between the German Empire and ourselves render such peril for the
time without foundation, in certain not
impossible events, coupled with any neglect
in our own watchfulness, it cannot be said
that the temptation for German intervention in South America, with its inevitable
results, would not present itself. It would

certainly be dangerous to interpret Germany's consulting us in her recent difficulties with Venezuela as an indication of her formal subscription to the Monroe Doctrine. The convenience of negotiation might cause her to treat with us repeatedly without further binding her to the recognition of any such principle. It may be well to recall Napoleon the Third's words to Slidell, that in diplomacy nothing was held to exist that had not formally been written. (Had M. Delcassé remembered this, he could not have made the mistake of believing that Germany assented to his Moroccan policy.) While any challenge of the Monroe Doctrine may safely be set aside so long as our naval strength makes us a formidable antagonist, it is doubtful if Germany or any other nation would attach importance to inferences which might be drawn from past acts, provided the existing incentive was adequate and the danger of action reduced to insignificant proportions. Unless a nation's hands are formally tied by written agreement, its acceptance of the Monroe or any other doctrine against its own interests cannot be presupposed.

The fear of Italian interference is fortunately very remote, and Italy's recent arbitration treaty with the Argentine proves the peaceful intentions of her present policy. Misfortunes in Abyssinia have for the time removed from her all taste for colonial ventures. But Italy, rapidly growing in national wealth and strength, wishes to regard herself as the successor of Imperial Rome. Her present policy is based on the preservation of existing conditions until such time as she may be better able to avail herself of opportunities. While the inflammable nature of her masses is to-day held in restraint by an able governing power, a real or fancied grievance suffered in a moment of violence by Italians in South America, such as once took place at New Orleans, might, without attention on our part, lead to consequences antagonistic to our policies. We cannot forget that in several of the South American

states, notably in the Argentine, the Italians
are the dominant foreign element, and that
the national *ethos* of the Latin republics is
not always strong enough to cause emigrants to forget the links that bind them to
the land of their origin. Fortunately the
many existing ties of friendship between
Italy and ourselves, which were strengthened
by the aid it was our privilege to extend
during the recent Messina disaster, render
most unlikely any difference between two
states possessing so many mutual sympathies.

The day may never come when either
Germany or Italy will seek to interfere in
the affairs of the southern continent. But
a nation, like the human body, acts differ-
ently under the stress of feverish excite-
ment. The wisdom of diplomacy lies in
removing possible causes of friction between countries during normal conditions.
It would be prudence to endeavor to secure from these powers at a time when
no popular passions have been aroused,

when neither national pride nor interests are at stake, and when only the friendliest relations exist between them and ourselves, a recognition of the principles underlying the Monroe Doctrine. If the acquiescence of Great Britain, France, and Russia were obtained, Italy would hardly care to place herself in opposition to subscribing thereto. And with the example of the other powers, Germany and her Austrian ally value our amity too greatly to take a position which could be interpreted as unfriendly. German diplomacy, realizing that such attitude on her part would tend to draw us closer to England, is far-sighted enough to accord her recognition in this event to our South American policies.

With the Monroe Doctrine thus officially recognized by the only powers in position to dispute it, its security would be as efficaciously guaranteed as by more aggressive means. Even were we otherwise unable to obtain such recognition, opportunities have not been wanting to secure it where we might have found the leverage necessary to effect diplomatic action. For instance, the United States had been invited to participate in the conference which met in 1885 to settle the future of the Congo and resulted in dividing the then unapportioned remainder of Central Africa. Our refusal to profit by its decisions, which our delegate had been instrumental in bringing about, may have been justified at a time when we were not yet a colonizing power; but the acquisition of even a tract of African jungle might have been of service later in securing, in exchange for its cession or lease to some more interested power, the recognition on its part of the Monroe Doctrine.

Certain more recent opportunities allowed to slip occurred during the Algeciras Conference. Germany on that occasion, in order to justify her position and give equity to a procedure the high-handedness of which did not escape the criticism of neutrals, had placed herself upon a self-denying basis and proclaimed as her intention

the laudable desire to safeguard the integrity of Morocco. Her position towards
that state was, with far less justification,
analogous to the one we occupy towards
South America. But in spite of the apparent justice of her contention, save for Austria, Germany could find for it no support
from any of the great European powers,
whose aid had, for different reasons, already
been pledged to France. Germany's efforts
were therefore directed to winning us over
to her side. As the only great power
enjoying complete freedom of action, our
rôle permitted considerable latitude. But
though its possibilities were wisely utilized,
our disinterestedness might, perhaps, have
been coupled with a vigilant diplomacy in
enlarging the scope of the German contention. Germany, professing eagerness to
preserve the integrity of Morocco as a field
of equal opportunity for all, would hardly
at the same time have acknowledged enter-
taining designs of a different order in the
western hemisphere. While her diploma-

tists were endeavoring to win us over to
their support, if a proposition had been
advanced aimed at guaranteeing the integrity of South America, in the same way
as Germany had put herself forward as the
champion of Morocco, it would have been
difficult for her to refuse us formal assur-
ances regarding the future of the Spanish
republics. A pledge thus secured might on
a later occasion have been an important
factor in the preservation of peace. The
hands of a nation are tied once it has made
official declarations; and though history
shows how conventions have been violated,
a country will be far more likely to abstain
from action when it has given pledges than
where none have been forthcoming. We
have only to remember how the French
omission to consult Germany in her Moroccan venture was utilized by the latter as
the excuse for an interference which brought
the two nations to the verge of war. By our
neglect to commit the Great Powers to a
recognition of the Monroe Doctrine, we

have lost a point in our favor which in a future period of strained relations might conceivably have swayed a wavering balance in the direction of peace.

Another opportunity occurred at the same conference in connection with the Moroccan state bank. Its foundation was exceptional in every way. But in semi-civilized states commerce and diplomacy are intimately connected. The bank share in question, to which we were entitled, was first accepted by us and then allowed to drop. The unprecedented inconvenience in the government's ownership of foreign bank stock, and the difficulties of its disposal to a private concern, are obvious. Representation, however, in the state bank of Morocco would have given us an entirely unexpected leverage to advance our commercial interests in that country, and have placed us on a footing of equality with nations far more directly concerned than ourselves. A less scrupulous diplomacy might, perhaps, have utilized such share for still another purpose. Even had it been of no immediate advantage to us, it would always have been so to a nation like France, possessed of special interests and ambitions in Morocco. And, although its direct control could not have been ceded to any foreign power, it is easy to imagine circumstances effecting the same purpose in return for equivalent advantages obtained elsewhere. The French possessions in the West Indies and off the St. Lawrence are now of little use to her, but would be of considerable importance to us. In the Moroccan bank share, which after having claimed we refused, there was lost to us a negotiable asset, so to speak, for the furtherance of our American policies.

We have not availed ourselves, in the past, of the natural diplomatic advantages which so often befall nations. We have been too self-centred over matters which appeared of more immediate concern, to have noticed distant events from which, without risk or loss, we might have profited. Similar opportunities unnecessary to mention, but where we could have gained substantial advantages, have arisen elsewhere; they are likely to occur again. The remedy lies with our diplomacy to prevent such chances from again being lost. By diplomacy as well as with battleships we can seek the advancement of our policies and the safeguarding of our possessions.

CHAPTER IV

THE LATIN REPUBLICS

THE victory of a republican movement parallel to our own, which resulted in liberating the greater part of the New World from the domination of the Old, could have been viewed by us only with sympathy. We welcomed as a complement to our own Revolution the success of the Spanish colonies in establishing their independence, both by reason of the extension given to the republican idea and because it removed so great a portion of the western hemisphere from the field of European politics.

The real beginning of our interest in Spanish America dates, however, from the declaration of the Monroe Doctrine. In proclaiming this we did not incur the risk of war with Europe merely because of friendship for struggling newborn states, or

for any abstract sentiment in favor of a form
of government which was frequently to become a cover for dictatorship. Our determination to resist any extension of foreign
influence was due to the nation's profound
conviction that its own vital interests would
thereby be imperiled. American foreign
policy has nowhere been more successful
than in securing the possibility for the New
World to develop free from European interference. But the celebrity achieved by
the Monroe Doctrine has obscured the real
nature of our intercourse with our southern
neighbors. Superficially the doctrine has
appeared to sum up the different aspects of
our diplomacy toward them. In reality it
has had but little to do with such relations.
In the past, present, and future it repre-
sents a permanent policy toward European
but not toward American states. Its relation to the latter may be likened to an outer
wall on which we have mounted guard to
permit their free development. Behind it
a series of American policies, moulded in

each case by the special exigencies of our position, still remains to be formed.

Our relations with the Spanish republics are far too diverse to be embraced by any single formula. Their varying geographical situation, even if no other cause were present, would necessarily be productive of different degrees of diplomatic interest on our part. Thus it is apparent that the Caribbean concerns us more intimately than the south Atlantic. Our policy in Cuba could manifestly not be repeated in Chili, while in Salvador we should act otherwise than in Paraguay. The foreign policy of any nation is dictated by its requirements, and the necessities of our position are far from uniform. But in a general way the Orinoco may be said to provide a natural division for our policies in South America. The interest we feel in the great states to the south of it, Brazil and the Argentine, is eminently one of disinterested friendliness, aiming principally to cultivate closer commercial intercourse. Moreover, the contemplated increase in the armaments of the larger South American republics, coupled with their growing importance as nations, bids fair in time to make these independent of our aid.

For the maintenance of such relations as we may wish to preserve with these states we must prepare other measures than a mere assertion of common Americanism. The bond that unites us is hardly more evident than is the Europeanism linking together a Norwegian and a Greek, and the amicable sentiments exchanged over toasts and telegrams rest on a fragile basis so long as our means of communication remain unimproved. It is difficult to convince the inhabitant of Buenos Ayres or of Rio de Janeiro of the proximity of mutual interests when, in order to reach North America, he finds himself obliged to go by way of Europe. A direct communication between our ports and theirs is as much a political as it is a commercial necessity. For our trade in almost every South American country, badly crippled by the present inadequate system, finds itself relegated to an inferior position. In order to justify the paramount title to which we lay claim in the Spanish republics, it still remains for us to prove the superiority of our interests to those of Great Britain, of Germany, and of France, whose capital has constructed most of their railways and financed their national and municipal loans

On the Pacific coast we are fortunately in better position. After developing Mexico, our engineers have descended into Central America, where the rails they are laying will one day serve as links for the Pan-American road. In Peru, and now in Bolivia, our enterprise has not been behindhand. But we have still considerable to accomplish to overtake the financial and industrial efforts of European powers in their South American enterprise.

Europe has long since awakened to the importance of Spanish America as a neutral market that will not soon be closed to the products of manufacturing countries. We, too, need anticipate there no discriminating tariff to bar our exports, while the increase of trade relations should be of mutual advantage. Our political interests can therefore be confined to the grateful task of assuming obligations without demanding corresponding equivalents. Our fleet is the pledge we extend to exclude the possibility of European interference. We need ask for nothing in return, since we desire nothing save the continuance of existing political conditions.

Our diplomacy has, however, to assert itself more emphatically in Venezuela, Colombia, and the West Indian and Central American republics, whose harbors command the approaches of the Panama Canal. The cutting of the isthmus and the new importance of the Pacific force us to realize that whatever consequence we formerly attached to the Caribbean has been immeasurably increased since the West Indies are to become a highroad to the Pacific, instead of a blind alley as heretofore. In determining the limits of our influence we must apply there what might be termed a Caribbean policy, in distinction from our relations with the other South American states, whose geographical situation renders them of less vital importance.

It is fortunate for us that the countries whose ports in unfriendly hands might prove a menace to us are debarred by their weakness from the possibility of taking offensive action. It is less fortunate that their weakness should not have constituted a pledge against their misconduct. Venezuela has so often in recent years ruffled by misdeeds the diplomatic calm of nations, that our solicitude in her behalf has arisen rather from the fear lest justifiable redress be sought from her by foreign powers whose action would necessarily take place in waters of peculiar importance to us. Both Venezuela and Colombia must always possess for us a special interest, due to their coast line, which assimilates them to the other Caribbean nations, while their close proximity to the isthmus makes it necessary at all cost to preserve their independence and guarantee their territory, even against themselves.

The two states enjoy an altogether anomalous situation, their position offering in certain respects an American analogy to the problem of the Dardanelles. In the same way that England has twice saved Turkey from dismemberment in order to prevent these straits from falling into the hands of a stronger power, it must be our object to preserve the inviolability of both countries, whatever be the provocation they give.

In connection with this, a word may be said of a frequent cause of dispute with the Latin republics, and particularly with Venezuela. Besides foreigners who possess perfectly legitimate business interests in Spanish America, there are others who, actuated by the hope of larger profits, employ more questionable methods. In return for special advantages or the expectation of future benefits, it often happens that they affiliate themselves unduly either with the government of to-day, who may be the revolutionaries of to-morrow, or the revolutionaries of to-day, who may be the government of to-morrow. In either instance, reprisals in the nature of fines or confiscations are likely to occur, and out of these grow claims for damages which our government as well as others has frequently been called upon to enforce. Such penalties, however, are nearly always imposed by decision of the country's highest court, which, outwardly at least, complies with the customary judicial forms.

It matters little that such courts are tools in a dictator's hands, and that legally their verdict may be questionable. If we opposed our own administrative judgment to their judicial authority, whatever might be our right in substance, we should, in view of the high, equitable stand we have always taken in such matters, err in form. Remedy exists, it is true, in the procedure of summary arbitration provided for by the recent Hague Conference, but this has still to prove its acceptability. It might be well, therefore, to prepare for contingencies of refusal, and either enlarge the jurisdiction of one of our own superior federal courts, or else establish a tribunal which might equitably apportion the extent and nature of claims of this nature prior to their being filed. Whatever be the legal competence of the State Department, its opinion in points of law cannot carry with it the same authority before the nation or before the world as would that of a properly constituted court. Moreover, since the efforts to adjudicate possible claims have necessarily to pass through diplomatic channels at some stage, it would be placing the governmental department concerned with foreign affairs in an unfair position, to demand that it both judge and enforce its judgment. Our diplomacy would escape much unnecessary and unjust criticism if, before pressing for the settlement of any claim against certain countries, we should insist on its first being examined and passed on by a competent tribunal. This accomplished, public opinion will judge as to the relative merit of our courts in comparison with those of states like Venezuela; but without this we lay ourselves open to the charge of having used violence to enforce doubtful claims against a weaker power.

While we could, if necessary, overrun or occupy without great impediment any of the West Indian or Central American states, our action in South America, were it ever to extend beyond the limits of diplomacy, would experience difficulty in going beyond the seizure of ports and the blocking of rivers. Hence Venezuela and Colombia stand in peculiar relation to our policy, enjoying practical invulnerability by nature of their continental position. Their highlands sloping from the coast mark the barrier we must impose as a southern limit to our active intervention.

Elsewhere in the Caribbean our position may be compared to that of the owner of a great estate surrounded by smaller neighbors. While disposed to leave these in undisturbed possession, should their property come into the market we should regard its acquisition prudent, to save it from falling into other hands. In Great Britain and, in lesser degree, in France, Holland, and Denmark, we have neighbors with whom our future relations are likely to be as sincerely cordial as are our present. We have neither incentive nor desire to disturb their actual colonial possessions. But if for any reason there should ever be the wish to dispose of these, we are not likely to repeat our former error in neglecting to acquire St. Thomas. And in case circumstances place us again in possession of territorial or diplomatic advantages in other regions of the globe, our statesmen may find therein useful pawns to offer in exchange for islands closer to our shores.

The nation's policy demands that we im-

pose in the Caribbean the *pax Americana*
by refusing to permit in it the turbulence
so often provocative of foreign interference.
In so doing, Porto Rico, Cuba, and San
Domingo offer the precedents for our future action. The one presents a final goal
toward which our policy must tend; the
others, intermediary stages in the same process. The possession of Porto Rico has
firmly established us as a West Indian
power, and our action in Cuba inaugurated
the beginning of a new policy toward the
islands within our national orbit. When
for the second time American intervention
had been invoked, the world marveled at
the political suicide Cuba was supposed to
have committed. It is characteristic of our
generosity that we pledged ourselves to re-
store the Cuban republic as soon as order
had been established, but we thereby likewise tied our hands' by an unexpected declaration and put off an almost inevitable
result. The laws of gravitation operate
with states as with planets, and the ultimate

future of Cuba can hardly be doubted.
Nor need our present forbearance be regretted if the American people learn from
it the necessity devolving upon them of
insuring stable government at their doors.
The long road we are now traveling in
Cuba in order to achieve a predestined result may serve at least to abridge later steps
when next a similar contingency presents
itself.

A different stage in our intervention is
now witnessed in San Domingo, where, with
no risk to ourselves, we are showing how
the muddled finances of a country can be
placed on a sound basis of credit, and have
the opportunity of acting in a disinterested
capacity without imposing an unwelcome
interference.

The justification of the European system of colonization over already populated
areas has always been that, whenever the
conditions of disorder in a country are such
that the principle of authority ceases to
exist and a menace is created to the life and

property of foreigners, this state of anarchy offers sufficient reason for the interference of a more powerful nation better capable of maintaining order. In the western hemisphere we have successfully opposed the Monroe Doctrine to such pretensions. But we should be lacking in equity if the result of our policy should be only to give a guarantee to the perpetuation of misrule and the freedom from molestation of a frequently irresponsible dictatorship. The justice of our position depends upon a firm determination to remedy, where we can, the flagrant abuses which would otherwise warrant foreign intervention; and since it is particularly in the region where our interests are most vital that certain states appear unable to maintain the requisite stability of government, it becomes our duty to assist these.

In Mexico we have to-day an orderly neighbor, the foundations of whose prosperity appear to be solidly laid. Our enterprise and capital have assisted largely in

furthering economic expansion south of the
Rio Grande. But to what extent the present conditions of order are due to the signal ability of its President, the retirement
of Diaz will alone prove. Has the genius of
a great statesman been sufficient to instill
habits of law-observance and a conception
of representative government in a country
unaccustomed thereto? The capacity of
Mexico as a modern state is a problem that
deeply concerns us, not only because it is
a neighboring country wherein we have
extensive interests, but because of the Central American republics. In the past we
have protected these from Mexican encroachments, and even less could we permit a change in their status now that they
have assumed an altogether new importance
by reason of the Panama Canal. Their
strategic position, commanding its northern
approaches on both the Caribbean and the
Pacific, is too great not to impose on our
policy the desirability of continuing the
present system of small independent states,

practically under our protection and over whom we are able to exert influence when necessary. The alternative would be their union with Mexico in what under a strong dictator might become a powerful nation, possibly antagonistic to our policies and able to invoke the intervention of foreign powers. This danger can be effectually prevented only by guaranteeing their present independence, a measure in line with our policy of years.

There exists traditionally what might be termed an unwritten corollary of the Monroe Doctrine, which demands that the American continent be not made the scene of such territorial partitions and seizures as have disgraced European warfare. And while we cannot lay claim to having followed this with strictness, the acquisition of California was that of a practically uninhabited territory, and not of a state which, however disorderly, was yet self-governing. Further land we neither seek nor require, save the lease of such coaling stations as

Amapala Bay on the west coast of Central America, the possession of which would offer the fleet a much-needed strategic base on the Pacific close to the canal, while our permanent retention of a small armed force at this junction of three turbulent republics would act as a wholesome restraint in curbing local revolution and assisting the maintenance of order.

A natural sympathy with the principle of arbitration has caused us to look favorably on the recent conference of Central American states held under our auspices. It is certainly to be desired that it fulfill the hopes of its promoters. But the fear may be expressed that these states are not yet ripe for the principles involved, and that by our assent we may have made ourselves party to a measure which will possibly deprive us later of means of action in correcting injustice when committed. Under existing conditions it would hardly be wise for us to curtail the assertion of our influence, and any forbearance in this direction out of respect for abstract principles would only be interpreted as a weakness which, in lands of such peculiar interest to us, might lead to fresh disturbances.

The southern limit of the United States is no longer the Rio Grande, but the Panama Canal, and although our territory is not unbroken, our influence should be. The Platt amendment, which mapped out our present policy in Cuba, offers a guiding precedent for future action in Central America. Nor is it believed by those best acquainted with the situation that any insurmountable difficulty would be met with in effecting its acceptance by the five republics. Therecognition of some such principle on the part of all the states bordering on the Caribbean would be a noteworthy achievement for our diplomacy. In any event, it is most important that our envoys should everywhere occupy in the Spanish republics a paramount position as friendly advisers to the governments to which they find themselves accredited. Their disinterested coun-

sel tactfully given in time could often obviate
entanglements with foreign powers and thus
relieve us from having recourse to possible measures as necessary as they would
be embarrassing. Such advice could be successful, however, only if the influence and
sense of equity of our envoys were to be
acknowledged by both sides. Our policy
should therefore aim at a most careful selection of diplomatic representatives who
would be acquainted, through long and special training, with the peculiar problems
they would be called on to handle. Moreover, it should endeavor to obtain for these
higher consideration by methods similar
to those employed by European powers
in the Orient. Just as other nations have
organized picked services for their representation in the Levant and in the Far
East, a like necessity impresses itself on us
in Latin America. But the organization of
such a body of men is insufficient without
giving it a prestige and advantages which
would make service of this nature prized

in spite of undoubted drawbacks in climate and life. The failure to provide advantages counterbalancing the hardships would only repeat the history of our student interpreters in China, where it has now been found necessary to remedy a condition which left within the service chiefly the inferior men, the abler ones abandoning it to accept more lucrative positions in commercial life. It would be no less shortsighted than unworthy of us as a nation, to endeavor to dole out with a sparing hand trifling benefits for arduous service of the nature we should expect.

The government ownership of suitable residences, and increases of pay in certain capitals, would do much to mitigate the present unpopularity from which Latin America suffers among diplomatists, while the former measure ought long ago to have commended itself, if on no other ground than as a national investment and a matter of national pride. The most important step is, however, for our representatives to enjoy when possible higher diplomatic rank than that of their colleagues. The European powers have been accustomed to send as their envoys to the Latin American countries ministers resident or plenipotentiary. In the same way France out of compliment to a sister republic sends an ambassador to Berne, our representative could in either instance be of a higher grade. Hence the recent amendment of the law on the creation of ambassadors was in certain respects unfortunate. Instead, for instance, of discouraging Chili from sending us an envoy of the highest rank, it would more likely have proved to our advantage to have had at Santiago an official of that grade, who by virtue of his grade would always have been dean of its diplomatic body.

As a nation we are disinclined to attaching significance to what would be irrelevant forms were it not for the importance attached thereto by other nations. With our habits of thought it is difficult to realize the advantage possessed by the dean of the diplomatic body not only in prestige, but in all questions involving concert of action. The Spanish republics, however, present a field where American diplomacy may often be at variance with that of the European powers, and if our envoy be dean, he could at times prevent possible concert on the part of the foreign representatives prejudicial to our interests. Conversely, it is not difficult to conceive of circumstances where a European dean might make use of his position and enlist his colleagues in a common action far from agreeable to us.

We have done so much to cultivate friendly relations with our southern neighbors in recent years that it is unfortunate our actions should at times have been misinterpreted. That a more correct appreciation of our motives should not invariably have existed, can in a certain measure be laid down at the door of diplomacy. In diplomatic intercourse with the South American states we have always to avoid the strictures of unfriendly criticism, remember-

ing that we have been regarded in the past
with a not unnatural fear and distrust by
the Latin republics lest the Monroe Doctrine afford a subtle means of drawing them
into our nets. Pan-Iberism has been opposed to Pan-Americanism; "Against Monroe we will pit Monroe and a half," a
Brazilian statesman is reported to have
said. In Chili especially an anti-American
movement had asserted itself, and the idea
was even mooted of a Latin American confederation, directed as much against us as
against the European powers.

Our policy of benevolent friendship has
not always been appreciated at its worth,
and we have found ourselves in the position
of having, without advantage to ourselves,
given unconscious offense to nations unable to retort and therefore hypersensitive
in their susceptibilities. A case in point
occurred during the recent Pan-American
Conference at Rio Janeiro. Our delegation
there was supposed to favor a so-called
"monitor" system, whereby it was intended

that the greater powers should exercise a general surveillance over the smaller countries in curbing their turbulent propensities and keeping the peace. While the intention underlying this was eminently proper and the result possibly beneficial, the differentiation thus suggested among Latin American states was not without giving offense to the weaker countries at such expression of their inferiority. Nor is it certain, even if there existed no risk of the larger powers seeking to abuse their position, that the latter would be better able to maintain order. The annals of Uruguay are perhaps as orderly as those of Brazil.

It is not difficult to see that the beneficial results of our policy in one quarter may be nullified by unintentional offense given elsewhere. Our interests are everywhere connected, and concerted action is no less necessary on the part of diplomacy than in other spheres. The recent Hague Conference provides further illustration of this. Our advocacy there of compulsory arbitration, while proving sympathy for humanitarian ideals, was not without imperiling the friendliness of relations with the Latin republics. Inseparably connected with the principle at stake was the creation of a court to judge questions of arbitration, and our pitfall, which to certain powers proved not unwelcome, lay in the composition of this tribunal. If the great European powers alone had been concerned, the solution would have been simple; but it was apparent that we could not expect these to allow questions of national interest to be decided by the judicial representatives of Ecuador and Paraguay. And while an ingenious compromise smoothed out the major difficulties of this thorny question, in view of our friendly feeling towards Latin America it might have been preferable for us to have expressed our adhesion to the plan of arbitration presented by some other nation rather than to have proposed it ourselves.

In spite, however, of certain easily remediable deficiencies, our relations with our southern neighbors, owing largely to the wise policy recently pursued with eminent success, have never been so cordial. And since our friendship is sincere and our interests are in no way divergent, there is every likelihood of the present amicable sentiments being continued.

Further than such friendship and our self-imposed unilateral obligation in defending the Monroe Doctrine it would be unwise for us to venture. The dream of a confederation of American republics headed by us, and leagued together in defense of common rights, would unfortunately be mainly impressive by the number of its states. It could not be regarded as a safe working basis for political action or military defense, nor would it find interest in our Asiatic dependencies. While such federation might prove of considerable utility under certain conditions, it would be rather as a secondary than as a primary basis for defense. An understanding, to be effective, can be contracted only with naval and colonial powers of the first magnitude, having interests similar to our own.

The instability of many of our southern neighbors offers both the cause of their weakness and the reason why we cannot blind ourselves to the responsibilities which may there devolve upon us. A skilled and watchful diplomacy maintained by us in these states, however, would contribute more than anything else in averting this danger and extending our legitimate influence without incurring the drawbacks of new and undesired possessions. We desire in Latin America only the furtherance of commercial ties and the preservation of their existing independence. In our own interest we can wish for no more.

CHAPTER V

OUR relations with the Far East have pursued a distinct course since the early days of the Republic when the enterprise of New England merchantmen first bore the flag into Chinese waters. In the struggle for commercial success in the Orient we were able to enter on an equal footing with the nations of Europe. In Japan we even preceded these and opened the Island Empire to the commerce of the world. American intercourse with the Far East stands thus on a different level from our foreign relations elsewhere. We have abstained from all interference in Europe, Africa, and the Levant, and rightly upheld preëminence on the American continent; in the extreme Orient our equality with the European powers has from the first been asserted. Geographically, politically, and economically alike, our interests predicated the position we have there assumed.

American policy in the extreme Orient has always been of a peaceful and commercial nature. Where Russia and France shaped for themselves colonial empires, where Germany, and even England, were ready to share in the spoils of an anticipated division of China, we have wisely abstained from similar attempts. We alone refrained from treating the Oriental nations in the same high-handed manner to which they were subjected at the hands of European powers. Rather have we given them abundant proof of the sincerity of our friendship and the equity of our conduct.

Even the acquisition of the Philippines, which made us an Asiatic power, did not alter previous relations, although forcing us to consider far more attentively problems that had before been remote. Our possession of the archipelago disturbed no balance of power, cut short no other ambitions than those of Filipino nationalism. We entertained no further territorial desires in the Far East, nor were likely ever to do so. Hence the amicable spirit which had characterized our former intercourse with China and Japan bade fair to be continued. We appeared to the Orientals as the one nation in whom they could place confidence, since we were devoid of political ambitions menacing their own.

There was thus no reason to anticipate that our Far Eastern interests need ever in the future clash with the legitimate aspirations of these powers. No fundamental differences severed us; certainly no differences of a nature necessitating violent solution.

Yet out of this clear sky, after a half century of the most cordial relations, and on the morrow of a period during which we had manifested more than usual friendship toward Japan, even at the cost of a traditional amity with Russia, there arose the talk of war. From a trifling matter of

school attendance the question was broad-
ened to that of mastery of the Pacific, and
sensation-mongers exploited that cry in
justification of their action. Fortunately
the governments of both nations realized
the wicked absurdity of a contest which
would have no object and would settle no
question. The Pacific is easily wide enough
for both Japan and America; no more than
the Atlantic can any one power now domi-
nate it.

That the shipping trade of the western
ocean is destined, in great measure, to fall
to the Japanese can hardly be doubted.
Their natural aptitude for the sea, coupled
with a cheap standard of wages and an inferior scale of living, renders their competition dangerous not only for us but for every
maritime power. The very few American
vessels plying the Pacific are notoriously
able to do so only by virtue of agreement
with the Japanese companies. Without this
they would soon be driven from the seas
unless provided with governmental sub-

sidies of more liberal nature than yet contemplated.

A war against Japan for the mastery of an ocean over which American vessels under normal conditions could not hope to sail, would thus offer but a sterile victory for our shipping. Moreover, it is hardly likely that either contestant could so completely crush the other as to secure its undisputed supremacy. Nor ought we to forget that a prosperous Japan, able to purchase our exports, is in many ways desirable to us. The commercial ties binding the two nations work for their mutual benefit, and the suffering of one cannot but react on the other. Fortunately, too many common interests exist for the diplomacies of both countries, instead of running counter, not to find it desirable to coöperate in neutral fields.

Even if Japanese protectionism be eventually applied to Korea, it cannot be easily enforced elsewhere upon the Asiatic mainland. We have sought to profit in the Far

East only by the open door of equal opportunity for all, and Japan has, with cause, pledged herself to the same programme. Possessed of abundant cheap skilled labor, resourceful and enterprising, she is already underselling her commercial rivals in many markets, and her industry has no need to fear the competition of the western nations.

The source of the present difficulties between the two countries is based rather on the white workingman's dread of the virtues and not the vices of the yellow races. The Pacific States intend to remain what has become vulgarly known as a "white man's country," with all the corollaries thereof which are likely to become multiplying thorns of trouble in proportion to the growing strength of Asiatic powers. Without entering into the moral or economic aspects of the question, we must well understand that henceforth our foreign policy will be obliged to accept this attitude as a fundamental condition for its action.

The problem is no new one. It is met

with in every land where a white self-governing community considers itself in danger through the economic competition of the
yellow races. The novelty of the present
situation arises from the fact that for the
first time an Asiatic state has found itself
in position to resent the discrimination and
insult to which its citizens have been subjected.

While the essential features of the question were, perhaps, unavoidable, in view of
the violence of opinion on this subject, a
similar result might have been accomplished
in California with, perhaps, less slight to
Japanese susceptibilities. We are, as a
people, too little conscious of the importance
of form, especially in dealing with a highly
sensitive and decorous Oriental race, among
whom politeness has passed into a second
nature. We frequently give offense where,
with a little care and under a slightly different form, the result aimed at could
have been otherwise attained. The refusal,
for instance, to permit Japanese pupils to

attend certain San Francisco schools was possibly justified. But such prohibition should have been general and not specific. Had all foreign children been excluded, discrimination could not have been alleged nor offense taken. Individual permission might later have been granted exceptionally, no matter in what numbers, and the same general purpose would thereby have been achieved if even a very few Japanese had been included in order to take the force out of their argument. Needless offense, however, was given, which more skillful handling could probably have greatly attenuated, even had it not altogether removed its ground. It is certain that any efforts on our part to avoid giving offense to the pride of the Japanese have been heartily appreciated and seconded by the Mikado's government, which desires the preservation of friendly relations as earnestly as does our own. Japan still owes us a debt of gratitude; and though a certain section of her public opinion may be trying to efface its remembrance by directing attention to present indignities, enough recollection of former friendship still remains to render unlikely any sudden revulsion.

If there is no reason to be pessimistic with regard to the future, undue optimism is hardly less dangerous. The present settlement of the immigration difficulties is of a strictly temporary nature. And while the Japanese government will for the present restrain emigration and continue to do so as long as it suits its convenience, the vital question at issue is kept in suspense and may at any time be reopened. Our policy has to take cognizance of these conditions, and our diplomatic position at its point of intersection between treaty and state rights has not yet achieved permanent results, nor established a broad harmonious foundation for our future relations with the Island Empire.

The success of negotiations between nations usually depends on the concessions which may be made by either side in return for proffered equivalents. We have been unduly generous in the past in bestowing diplomatic favors without obtaining or even asking compensation. It is true that when, in 1894, we abandoned our extra-territorial privileges in Japan we obtained the treaty right to regulate the emigration of laborers, upon which rests the justice of our present contention. But this right was not so clearly indicated and defined as might have been desirable, although at that time we could more easily have secured concessions than is possible to-day.

Even during the late Russian war the more than benevolent neutrality and sympathy shown by us toward the Japanese, and the later abandonment of our legation at Seoul, which we were the first to give up in spite of our great interests in Korea, were favors freely granted without return. However proper may have been our action in so doing — and generosity on the part of nations is not always an unwise policy — it is conceivable that, had compensation been demanded, it would have been to Japan's interest, at a time when her national energies were engaged in a great war, to have made us concessions which might have prevented the present difficulties from arising. Instead, we have lately found ourselves in a position where negotiations became necessary, and asking for favors when we had no longer any to offer in exchange.

The demonstration made by our fleet's cruise to the Pacific and thence around the world has proved an act of audacious foresight. It is a commonplace to say that the surest guarantee for future peace is the maintenance of so large an armed strength as not to make it worth another nation's while to disturb it.

But the Tokio government, however desirous to avoid war, was more likely to turn a deaf ear to possible popular clamor when conscious of the magnitude of its risk than in the case of an enterprise presenting no peril, while bellicose clamor on the part of the masses was also less likely to arise.

Frank recognition of the danger of war is a more certain means of preventing its occurrence than the refusal to admit such possibility. Such danger as exists to-day lies in chance incidents taking place on either side, as unfortunate as they may be unforeseen. The violence of a mob, the act of a lunatic, is sufficient, once popular passions have been aroused. And we cannot afford to forget that in the event of conflict our most vulnerable spots would be Hawaii, where more than half the population is Japanese; Alaska, which in its remoteness and uninhabited condition presents points of danger like another Saghalien to Russia; and the Philippines. With regard to the latter especially, the position of Japan would not be dissimilar to our own at the outbreak of the Spanish War. We had then no wish for the islands which force of circumstances were to place in our possession. To-day the Japanese assure us in all good faith how remote is their desire to possess them. Nor have we reason to doubt their word. Japan's hands are tied in Korea, where a sullenly hostile population has caused them unforeseen difficulties. In Manchuria and China their course has been far from smooth, and the pugnacious insistency of the latter power in questions of Manchurian jurisdiction and other matters has afforded unexpected surprises. With Formosa barely pacified, any effort to acquire the Philippines would involve further drain on their already strained resources at a time when they are traversing a financial crisis and have to face budgetary troubles. Moreover, the issue of the war, in view of our present superior naval strength, would presumably be favorable to us. On our side there certainly exists no desire to spur it on. While Japan, as was proved by the peace of Shimonoseki, will for years smother insults until strong enough to avenge them, yet in spite of weighty considerations the future may cause present probabilities of peace to alter. The actual disparity in favor of our sea power will not long

continue without greater efforts on our part.
Nor can we forget that the failure of Japan
to secure the much-coveted indemnity in her
recent war was attributed largely to our intervention in the restoration of peace. The
capture of any of our territory in the event
of hostilities might easily appear to the
Japanese imagination as a surety to be retained in pledge for an indemnity of which
we had previously deprived them.

Although ominous clouds impend, danger will be remote if we do not neglect the
natural advantages of our position, diplomatic as well as military. We have in
the past willingly entered into coöperation
with other powers in sanitary matters of
mutual interest. A similar course com-
mends itself in questions of emigration.
The position of Australia, of New Zealand,
and of western Canada in refusing Japanese
coolie labor is in such matters entirely analogous to our own. In Australia the laws
restricting Asiatic immigration are, if possible, even more stringent than ours. But the

gravity of the situation created by such hostility has impressed itself upon the commonwealth. Mr. Deakin's recent compulsory service measures, aiming to create a nation trained to arms, prove that his government fully realizes its responsibilities with regard to the dangers resulting from the attitude assumed.

If only for future contingencies, we should seek closer interchange of views upon similar matters with the great self-governing British colonies bordering on the Pacific. Among obvious measures which commend themselves would be the appointment of consuls-general at Melbourne, at Wellington, and at Ottawa, who should be diplomatic officers, in the same way that European governments send diplomatists as consuls to such capitals as Budapest and Calcutta. Our interests are too identical not to be mutually reënforced. Nor could Great Britain regard otherwise than favorably the increase of our intimacy with her colonies, since measures concerted

in common would add to the weight of any
arguments that the course of diplomatic
negotiations might bring forth. By making general the interest of any question, it
would be plain to Japanese statesmen that
wherever their position might be contrary
to ours it would likewise be opposed to that
of their ally's colonies.

The necessity for taking such precautions
arises, however, from our acquisition of the
Philippines. Had we not these to defend,
Japan would have been almost powerless
against us. Possessing them, a different
course of action imposes itself which bids
us seek an understanding with Great Britain
to maintain existing conditions and join in
a mutual guarantee for the preservation
thereof, a guarantee which it is likely
enough that Japan, realizing her consequent impotence and desiring to identify
herself with the other Great Powers, would
herself subscribe to, as she lately has for the
French colonies in Indo-China; for Japan
diplomatically isolated would be powerless.

The alliance between England and Japan may not be of indefinite duration. The mutual desire to resist Russian encroachments in China, which originally brought it about, now appears removed, and already conflicting interests and prejudices caused by Great Britain's imperial position seem prepared to assert themselves. The prestige justly gained by Japan through her recent war has extended over Asia, where populations once submissive have had instilled in them novel ideas of independence. However remote it may be from the minds of Japanese statesmen to profit by the new feeling of unrest which has made itself felt in India, it would be only human if consciousness thereof were coupled with any resentment that might be felt for the humiliation suffered by their compatriots in British colonies. This feeling would naturally tend to loosen the bonds of an alliance which has more than accomplished the purpose for which it was originally intended.

The future may well witness Japanese

friendship inclining toward a nation like
Germany. The essentially military fabric
of both countries offers points of sympathy
which receive support from the fact that no
divergent interests separate the two powers,
while many draw them together, notably the common dread of Russia. Now
that all hope of establishing a German colonial empire in China has been abandoned,
and her colony at Kiauchau remains like a
beached vessel to mark the force of the wave
which stranded it, there are no longer rival
ambitions to clash.

In spite of his early warnings against
the yellow peril, the German Emperor has
every reason to feel as much sympathy
for the Japanese as for the Mohammedans,
to whom he once announced his all-em-
bracing friendship. Japan is better worth
German unity than Morocco, and an alliance with her could be heralded as offering
further guarantees for the preservation of
peace. But we could not afford to regard
this contingency with indifference. Should

it ever approach consummation, German
ambitions with regard to the Philippines
may again be awakened under a more formidable guise, and in such event any course
for us other than a prompt understanding
with Great Britain is likely to be disastrous
to the preservation of our dependencies.
Even without this possibility, which fortunately still belongs to the future, England
provides for us the effective means of safeguarding the possession of our colonies and
forestalling the peril which unfriendly combinations of powers present for us.

In lesser degree our diplomacy may de-
rive much benefit in strengthening our
Asiatic position by a frank understanding
with Russia. Now that the latter's Far
Eastern ambitions have been curtailed, the
two nations can find mutual advantage in
upholding a defensive policy aimed at the
preservation of existing conditions. Our
interests are mutual in so many respects
that a far-sighted policy would, perhaps,
even waive the assertion of certain claims,

however justified they may be, in return for
a friendship of greater importance to the
future of our position. Japan would hesi-
tate in the assertion of any pretension on
her part if she felt that we were assured of
the joint support of Great Britain and
Russia. Hence our desire to recognize
Chinese sovereignty over Manchuria should
take Russian ambitions into consideration.
Especially at the present time, when that
power is unable to assert an aggressive
policy, such action on our part would be
appreciated far more than it would have
been a few years ago, or is likely ever to be
in the future. It rests with our diplomacy
to profit by opportunities when they are
best worth seizing. The Far East is to us
what the Levant has been to the European
powers. In China our commerce has been
intrenched by a century of effort. Mer-
chants and missionaries have extended
American enterprise throughout that empire, while at home our educational institutions have been freely opened to Oriental

students. We cannot, therefore, regard with indifference the impending industrial awakening of China. Our energy and our capital have every right to participate therein at least on terms of equal footing with those of other powers; and the recent efforts of American diplomacy to support the assertion of such right in the matter of a railway concession offer a welcome sign that the nation is awakening to the growing importance of our over-sea interests, particularly in the Far East. Within late years we have taken a leading part both in virtually defeating the desired apportionment of the Chinese Empire into rival spheres of so-called economic development and influence, and in forcing on other reluctant nations the policy of the "open door." It has rightly been our aim to preserve the Chinese markets open for all. We should continue to assert vigorously in the Far East a policy in conformity with the principles of equity and our own best interests, which in Asia are commercial and cannot be political.

We should especially seek to continue to play a leading part as a friendly adviser of China. Nor ought this to be difficult. Our political friendship has been manifested on frequent occasions, although the late repayment of the exaggerated indemnity claims made after the Boxer rising was but the correction of a former injustice, an example which other powers have not seen fit to follow. The recent developing of our Chinese service, and our creating a body of student interpreters from whose ranks it is hoped that future consuls in the Far East will be recruited, offer an indication of the increasing importance the Orient has rightly assumed in our foreign relations. It is to be hoped that every effort will be made to strengthen the prestige of our representation which counts for so much in the East.

But if we have befriended China politically, in other questions our action has been less amicable. Even though we need fear no military consequence of her possible displeasure, the humiliation imposed upon Chi-

nese in America has in recent years caused
a boycott of our goods extending even to
Singapore. With China, just as with Japan,
tactful means should be found which would
accomplish the result demanded by our
labor in the Pacific States in a manner less
offensive to Oriental dignity. Fortunately,
a marked improvement has lately been witnessed in our relations with China, to which
the present resentment felt by that country
at the high-handed methods of Japan is
perhaps not foreign. This cannot be altogether disagreeable to us; and it should be
the constant object of our diplomacy, even
at the risk of seeming inconsistency, to avoid
uniting the two great yellow powers by fur-
nishing them with a common grievance.

Our policy in the Far East thus finds itself limited by certain existing factors imposed by labor conditions and over which
diplomacy has but a feeble control. Since
they exist, however, a course of action
becomes necessary for present and future
intercourse. To extend our commercial in-

terests, and to preserve the Philippines pending the decision with regard to their ultimate fate, must be our purpose. The goal toward which our diplomacy should strive is to mitigate as far as possible the offense given by exclusion acts, while so intrenching our position as to minimize the risk of its ever being challenged.

CHAPTER VI

THE NEAR EAST

EVEN before the recent revolution in Turkey, a decided revival of diplomatic interest in the affairs of the Near East had begun to be apparent. The conditions of disorder which so often in the past had furnished there the pretext for foreign interference appeared more ominous when the danger clouds were for the time dissipated in other regions of the globe. A feeling of unrest leading to violence and anarchy had further spread over the Moslem countries from Morocco to Afghanistan. Never tranquil even in orderly times, their chronic turbulence was once more excited. The East was beginning to appreciate the failure of Mohammedan institutions to renovate themselves in conformity with modern requirements, and its intelligence was realizing

keenly the inferiority from which it suffered. A political seething connected with
the idea of nationality and the victory of an
Asiatic over a European power, and influ-
enced by the constitutional struggle in Russia, became everywhere apparent. Western
forecasts regarding Oriental immutability
were rapidly being disproved.

Although almost our first foreign conflict
had been with the Barbary States, tradition
and interests alike would on the surface
seem to counsel us aloofness from the Mohammedan countries. Having voluntarily
refrained from whatever might entangle
us in the internal affairs of Europe, how
much more remote must appear the internal affairs of the Near East! Such arguments would have been irrefutable before
the Spanish War, and would still be so if
our international position had remained
unchanged and we could feel certain of
preserving our former policy without refer-
ence to the exigencies of a new situation.
But the diplomatic action of a great power

is everywhere too closely interwoven to be separate and distinct in each country. A purely defensive diplomacy on the part of a great state is as much a heresy as is a navy built only for defense.

The acute interest taken by the European nations in Turkish affairs has been not only because of political and commercial opportunities there open, but also because the problem of an empire's dismemberment, which for so long seemingly presented itself as imminent, caused the statesmen of the Old World to realize that without the greatest circumspection in their action a conflagration might be lit over the division of the spoils, setting all Europe ablaze. Even though we may regard the Near Eastern question as entirely foreign to us, it can hardly be anticipated that a European war resulting from it and upsetting all former balances of power could leave us completely indifferent. Our desire to avert such danger is in fact second only to that of the Old World powers. It behooves us as well as them to take the proper precautions toward removing such causes as tend to disturb the peace. Although we may not choose to forfeit our independence of action by entering into present or future concerts of nations, American policy can no longer, as in the past, afford to be oblivious thereto. Seen in this light, the joint action of the Powers in the Near East, which for thirty years has contributed largely to maintaining peace if only by isolating its occasional conflicts, assumes new importance for us. We can hardly disinterest ourselves with impunity from events in a region where the interests of other nations with whom we are elsewhere intimately connected are in such close juxtaposition. The Near East is at one door of Europe and we are at the other. The distance is too slight to leave us unconscious of our neighborhood.

In this connection another possibility presents itself as a living problem, even though to-day its contingency is remote. Only a few months ago, however, it looked

as if a new congress might become necessary
to revise the threadworn Treaty of Berlin.
Had this occurred, as the questions it
would have been called upon to regulate
are of wider than strictly European order,
and as its aim would lie in the direction of
permanently establishing the bases of international harmony, we could not have been
indifferent to its deliberations. Any effort
towards the preservation of peace in any
region of the world concerns us as well as
Europe. It matters little that we have no
direct interest in determining the status of
territories formerly under Ottoman suze-
rainty. We feel a very deep interest, first, in
any measure contributing to securing uni-
versal peace, and secondly, that no concert
of nations should meet to decide questions
of more than particular or local interest in
any portion of the world without taking our
views into consideration.

Public opinion in the United States
should distinguish sharply between spheres
of influence with regard to our foreign

policy and spheres of interest. There exist
many regions of the globe where any acquisition of territory, or single responsibility,
would prove only an encumbrance for us.
But there is none where we do not feel
interested, however remotely.

Our special right to participate in any
international deliberations modifying or
altering in any way the status of the Ottoman Empire is based, moreover, on the
existing treaties we possess with Turkey,
which cannot be changed without the consent of the contracting powers. Hence any
alteration in the legal status of such territory would almost inevitably entail a corresponding modification of the numerous
rights emanating from the ancient capitula-
tions which we have assimilated by virtue
of our treaties with the Sublime Porte. And
while we may be indifferent to surrendering
these, we cannot permit their abrogation to
be effected by other powers without our
consent, unless at the same time we are willing to permit other remaining rights, as well

as our international prestige, to be seriously jeopardized by such surrender.

Although in 1878 our position as a great power was still not sufficiently established to warrant a representation at the Congress of Berlin, American over-sea interests have since been so enlarged, American influence so universally recognized, that we could not absent ourselves from another such conference without endangering our legitimate influence in the world's affairs. Participation would not, however, mean our being dragged into acquisitions of undesirable or indefensible territory. Certainly no Cyprus nor Bosnia should tempt us or distract our attention. Like France at Berlin in 1878, it should be our boast to leave such a conference with empty hands. Nor again would such participation by us mean entanglement in the internal affairs of European states. We have as little wish to so enmesh ourselves as a century ago. But we are unable to permit questions not of internal but of international order, which might endanger the peace of other powers with whom we are intimately connected, to be decided entirely apart from our knowledge and consent, without surrendering just so much of our influence as the question's importance in its international aspects may involve.

It should further be our boast to employ the Republic's efforts wherever possible in the direction of justice and the extension of liberal ideas. To possess a true meaning in the world, our influence and civilization must not remain confined to a single hemisphere. Though its paramountcy in both the Americas has rightly been the cardinal point in our foreign policy, there is no reason why it should be restricted thereto. To refrain timidly from elsewhere asserting ourselves will not add one iota to the strength of our position in the western hemisphere, where our claims repose on no other ultimate basis than that of force.

But if a nation's hegemony can be asserted only with the adequate backing of strength, its pretensions to equality with other powers, especially when disinterested, may rest on more moral grounds. If the direction of our foreign policy in other regions of the world bears an ideal of justice in view, there is no reason why our influence, earning the respect due to its unselfishness, should not contribute toward the advancement of those general ideas of humanity and international morality with which we have always sympathized. And with the growth of our influence abroad will follow the extension of commercial interests in regions before unknown. All these causes contribute to the utility of our taking part in future international conferences and exchanges of opinion, where our presence, particularly to Great Britain and France, would be welcome, while it is doubtful if any power would care deliberately to choose to incur our displeasure by opposing our admission to the councils of great nations.

Paradoxical as it may appear, the student

of our national growth can hardly avoid the
conclusion that just as our former weakness,
with its dangers limited to a continent distant from the rest of the world, had been
our strength, our present strength, with the
new responsibilities thrust upon us, and
the rightly felt ambition to achieve great
deeds, has proved a source of weakness to
our material if not to our moral position.
It is curious to observe that the vast extension given within recent years to the international influence of the United States
and to our supposed designs in other continents, which abroad has attracted so much
attention, has yet passed almost unnoticed
at home, because of the slight consideration
accorded to questions of foreign policy.
The European nations, with keener sense of
the scope of diplomacy, long since perceived
the significance of our advent as a great
power. Almost unknown to us we have
been included in their new world-balance
which has replaced the former continental
equilibrium. Indeed, our foreign move-

ments are scanned abroad with far more
critical attention than they receive in
America.

A case in point occurred in 1906 in the
elevation of our legation at Constantinople
to the grade of an embassy. The importance of this measure passed almost unnoticed at home. But the ill-will it provoked,
especially in a certain section of the continental press, proved the consequence
attached by the Old World to a step interpreted as marking the entrance of America
in the Near Eastern question. Europe,
which jealously feared the appearance of
another claimant in the then anticipated
division of the spoils, realized the opportunity awaiting us in the Levant, where with
no political traditions to continue, no stakes
to defend, no territorial ambitions, entirely
unpledged and free in our actions, a skillful
diplomacy could win for us on the Bospho-
rus the recognition of our policies in other
quarters.

The success of our position in Constanti-

nople was fortunately never predicated on
the dismemberment of the Ottoman Empire.
We had no desire to see it divided, nor to
watch its provinces gradually apportioned
among the neighboring powers. It has always been to our advantage to have Turkey
preserved as one of the few neutral markets
still open to the world, where a fair field could
but be favorable to our foreign trade. Va-
rious conditions, past and present, have con-
spired together to prevent it from becoming
a manufacturing state. For many years
to come we need expect there no prohib-
itive tariff to bar our products, such as pro-
tects foreign markets and our own, while
the alienation of Ottoman territory would
have meant its probable inclusion within
the customs wall of some foreign power.

Our interests therefore coincided with
those of the powers desiring the preservation of Turkey. But not even her best
friends believed it possible long to avert the
doom which had appeared imminent. The
revolution of July, 1908, exploded like a

bombshell to astonish the world and open a new chapter in the Near Eastern question. By its promise to make of Turkey a modern state in place of a decrepit despotism, it held forth the vision of a regenerated nation. The European powers, some in all sincerity, others not wishing to appear unfriendly, welcomed the advent of a constitutional government. The empire which for two centuries diplomatists have regarded as the peculiar field for the exercise of their talents of division, appeared by a miracle of miracles to embark on a new life. For a moment it seemed as if the bond of Ottoman nationality founded upon the love for a common soil might henceforth unite without dissension the many creeds and races inhabiting Turkey, and bring to an end the conflict of racial ambitions fostered from without, which had made it a menace to the peace of Europe.

To-day, a year after the establishment of constitutional government, if the aspirations of the leaders of the new movement in

Turkey are in certain respects less generous, they rest, perhaps, upon a stronger
foundation. The success of the revolution
had been too sudden and overwhelming.
It had not to fight its way against a gradually receding opposition, but triumphed
almost at its birth. The elements of reac-
tion later made themselves felt with the realization that the heritage of long years of
misgovernment could not be shaken off in a
day. A band of young enthusiasts, many of
them bred in exile, and without practical
experience, found themselves at the head
of a nation to govern which presented the
most difficult problems of statesmanship,
from without as much as from within. The
ambitions of neighboring powers, the conflict of races and religions, the ignorance of
the masses, the ruined finances, an ineffi-
cient and frequently corrupt bureaucracy,
were all elements to be reckoned with; and
the fact that as each problem had been
the product of years, it was impossible to
solve it in a day, has caused many to be

unduly pessimistic regarding the future of
Turkey.

There is no reason, however, to take such
a dismal view of the situation. The necessary transition between the old order and
the new will hardly be effected without
many anxious moments. But the patriotism of the leaders of the reform movement
in Turkey, and particularly the devotion
to the constitutional cause of a disciplined
and highly efficient army composed of the
best elements in the nation, make one hope-
ful that a land so richly endowed by nature, and whose dominant race is possessed
of so many military and other virtues, will
in time again assume its rightful place in
the world.

We can view with warm sympathy the
successive steps in the evolution through
which Turkey must necessarily pass to accomplish this desired result. We can even,
without prejudice to ourselves, extend it
valuable aid when the proper time comes,
by abandoning, as in Japan, the special

rights of jurisdiction formerly acquired by treaty, and aid a new Turkey, in the measure of our ability, to extricate itself from one of the burdens of its inheritance derogatory to its sovereign rights.

The existence of a liberal Turkey is welcome to us both on sentimental and on material grounds. We should, indeed, prove unfaithful to our most ancient and most generous traditions if we failed to view with cordial satisfaction the success of a movement securing liberty, equality, and justice to a people hitherto deprived of the most elementary guarantees of government. Because our history has served as a guide for other nations in their fight for freedom, they look toward us for sympathy in their period of struggle and for friendship in their success. When on the morrow of the promulgation of the constitution the crowd in the streets of Constantinople cheered the American flag; when a marshal of the empire, the victorious hero of a former war, returning amid the enthusiastic demonstrations of the multitude from an unjust exile, paid his first visit to the American ambassador as a tribute to the representative of a nation which had been a cradle of liberty and a refuge for the oppressed, it was because we are regarded as possessing fundamental feelings and traditions which must cause us to welcome the success of other nations who have followed our example in the desire for representative institutions. We have thus to fulfill a generous and pleasing rôle in no way contrary to our real interests.

At the present time, when the demolition of the old order in Turkey causes every European nation to give an altogether fresh direction to its Near Eastern policy, we are able to enter on an equal footing with other powers in availing ourselves of the opportunities certain to arise with the industrial awakening of the Ottoman Empire. The system is fortunately shattered which in the past debarred from participation those who scrupled in their choice of methods. There is no longer to be the same disgrace-

ful scrambling for concessions purchased
through palace favorites which stained
those who were most successful. A policy
of equal opportunity for all will permit our
enterprise to profit legitimately in what is,
perhaps, the richest of undeveloped nations.
Hence interest with sentiment counsels our
viewing favorably the new government
which in saving Turkey from dismemberment has preserved it as an open market for
the commerce of the world.

So long as all our energy and capital were
engaged in developing the United States,
we had regarded foreign lands rather as
convenient dumping-grounds for our sur-
plus products than as countries where our
industrial and financial influence could be
continuously felt. Save along the Pacific
coast and to a certain extent in the Caribbean, the possibilities of great engineering
works, the building of harbors and bridges
and railways, the equipping of lighting, tele-
phone, and industrial plants, hardly dawned
upon our enterprise, while the possibili-

ties of financial operations abroad, and particularly in extra-territorial countries, were still uncontemplated. If it has not been already reached, we are likely in the near future to attain a stage where, the consuming capacity of the country being reduced, there will come a plethora of production and of unemployed capital. It may even be said that the recent industrial depression in the United States would have been less acute if its foreign trade had been greater and more widely distributed. The gigantic strides taken at home in recent years, however, have kept us from cultivating till quite lately over-sea outlets for our production in the same way as other powers have done. Now that an impetus has at last been given to export trade, we are likely to find other interests strongly intrenched in neutral markets, and our competitors appearing more formidable than would have been the case if our efforts to undersell them had been ripened by the experience of years. But in any event, our best openings will certainly be found in lands where no discriminating tariffs exist to favor home industry.

The preservation of the Moslem nations as a fair field for all assumes fresh importance for us because of this. And the Near East presents enough commercial attractions to warrant its receiving far closer attention from our trade. The European nations have better understood this advantage in the Levant, where they have strained every effort to secure the concession of public franchises. In the Orient, where commercial enterprise invariably passes through official channels, diplomacy has to concern itself with questions it elsewhere ignores. German diplomacy was the first to recognize this, and it was due largely to its able efforts that German interests in the past became so strongly intrenched in the Ottoman Empire. Our own commerce and enterprise, in spite of occupying a naturally favorable position to extend American trade and industry, has practically neglected a field where, only a few years ago, our exports were not one twentieth those of Belgium. It is interesting to note that one of the causes contributing to the success of Belgian diplomacy in securing valuable concessions in foreign countries has been that nation's political weakness. American enterprise would be similarly benefited by our remoteness and disinterestedness as a nation.

Our participation in industrial competition would be welcomed by a government aiming to distribute its favors widely and realizing that we possess no territorial ambitions over the Turkish Empire. The rich grants from which in recent years German capital has benefited in Anatolia and Mesopotamia, British in the Aidin Valley, and French in Syria, are by no means exhausted. Thousands of miles of railway remain to be built and railway material to be ordered. The whole northern portion of Asia Minor and the fertile valleys of the centre are still destitute of adequate means of com-

munication, although it is notorious that
such a road would traverse the richest part
of Turkey. The reason why it was left un-
built will also serve as an example to explain
the chance for our enterprise to profit from
the peculiar political position we enjoy in the
Near East. The first route for the Bagdad
Railroad had been planned to pass through
this region. But Russia, unwilling to see
the interests of a powerful nation permanently established close to her own Cauca-
sian frontiers, and in a district over which
she was supposed to cherish ultimate ambitions, demanded the immediate repayment
of the remainder of the Turkish war indemnity owing her since 1878. As this was impossible, she obtained instead the guarantee
for such road to be built either by Russian
or Turkish enterprise, while the Sultan re-
scinded his first offer and granted the German concession by the less favorable route
through the Taurus Mountains, and thence
across the semi-desert from Aleppo to Bagdad. The reasons which animated Russia

to take such a position would not be so
likely to militate against American interests. Hence our very aloofness from political ambitions in the East should stand us in
good stead. In the numerous concessions
for public franchises of every nature which
still remain to be granted in the Near Eastern countries, while we may anticipate commercial rivalry, our enterprise will hardly
suffer from political jealousy. On the contrary, we should obtain the aid in such ventures of a nation like Russia, which, without
the ability to profit commercially herself,
would prefer to see our interests benefited
rather than those of other powers. In the
Near East almost as much as in the extreme
Orient our interests may work in harmony
with those of Russia.

Opportunities thus await American capital and commerce in the Levant which may
be further increased by judicious means.
The establishment of schools in the Orient
has offered a recognized method of extending the national influence of powers so doing.

Without governmental aid American missionary establishments scattered throughout Turkey have accomplished the same purpose and extended among natives the use of the English language. Their utility could in certain respects be still further augmented. Many members of our chambers of commerce contribute in their private capacity to the support of the missions abroad. It would appear to be supplementing the influence and usefulness of the latter if a means of coöperation could be found whereby selected mission pupils would be assured a livelihood in advancing American trade interests. In addition to the instruction now imparted, commercial courses might be given which would prepare scholars as competent agents for our business enterprises. Among the present hindrances to the extension of American trade in the Levant is the absence of properly equipped natives who alone can push it in the interior. In our mission schools, which already accomplish much useful and beneficial work,

we possess the nucleus at hand to remedy
this deficiency. Next to Turkey, and in spite
of its present anarchy, Persia offers the most
attractive outlook in the commercial future
of the Near East, as an almost entirely undeveloped country possessed of natural resources, where only the most rudimentary
means of transportation and communication exist, and where possibilities of the
same character as in the Ottoman Empire
await foreign enterprise. In a land where
the dominant influence is that of Russia
in the north and England in the south,
we should be able to advance our commercial interests without incurring the
political jealousy of two powers that are
friendly toward us. The recent Anglo-
Russian agreement stipulated that central
Persia should be left as a zone between the
spheres of influence of either nation. There
can be no question that both England and
Russia would choose to see American interests established in this buffer region in preference to those of other likely powers.

The scope and direction for our diplomacy
is therefore apparent, if our enterprise and
capital can be induced to venture into this
new field and reap the benefits which freedom from political ambitions should obtain
for us.

While geographically far removed from
the Near East, the conditions prevailing
in Morocco align it with other Mohammedan countries as a non-manufacturing
state with yet undeveloped resources. Although recent events have partly removed
it from the strife of political competition,
while the state of anarchy in which the country has been plunged during late years
has made the extension of any commerce
almost impossible, there is reason to anticipate that greater tranquillity may in the
future prevail and peace be restored to a
distracted land. The guarantee of a fair
field for all nations was among the most
fortunate achievements of the Algeciras
Conference, although we unfortunately refused to avail ourselves of the proffered

share in the state bank of Morocco, which would have secured for us a favorable position to exert influence in behalf of American enterprise. But proper diplomatic support may yet place us on an equal footing with other states in the future award of public works and the distribution of concessions.

Our diplomacy skillfully handled can perhaps still find in Morocco a pawn to be utilized for advantages to be gained in other quarters. We need only remember the compensations secured by Great Britain, Italy, and Spain in surrendering to France their more or less shadowy Moroccan claims, to realize that, possibly, even at this late hour, we can secure certain advantages from the latter power in regions of closer interest to us, while, without injury to ourselves, we further possess the welcome opportunity of being of service to Spain in her special ambitions over northern Morocco.

The Near East is by no means the remote region it has so long seemed to us. Diplomatically and commercially, advantages are

there presented which in the past we have
been slow to cultivate. It is natural that
Europe should have forestalled us in fos-
tering relations with the Moslem powers;
but for us longer to neglect the opportunities there open, and allow our diplomatic
and trade intercourse with the Levant to
continue in its present undeveloped state,
is unworthy of a great and ambitious nation. With the extension everywhere given
to the protective-tariff system, the few neutral markets remaining will be increasingly
prized. Turkey, Persia, and Morocco offer
lucrative opportunities to our enterprise
and to the extension of our influence. We
are still in time to profit by the possibilities
there open, while the natural advantages
we enjoy by reason of our remoteness and
political disinterestedness place us in a pe-
culiarly favorable position to find support
for our policies, and aid for our industrial
enterprises in lands where our advent would
be welcomed in preference to that of other
powers.

CHAPTER VII

THE DIPLOMATIC SERVICE AND THE STATE DEPARTMENT

THE brains and energy of the nation have been largely absorbed, during the last century, by its industrial expansion. Whereas in the Old World they went by preference to the service of the State, with us they have gone rather into business life. The insecurity of government employment was able to offer but a scanty equivalent for the prizes awarded to success in industry and commerce. Public services stagnated while in all other directions the current of progress bore the country swiftly along. The fundamental reason for any inferiority in our governmental efficiency has been the political nature of its recruitment, with the resulting conditions little conducive to permanence or training. The disadvantage of utilizing national services as instruments of political reward, even though native talent has occasionally compensated for lack of experience, requires no comment here. For diplomacy, however, there has been and still is a certain justification. Apart from our scarcity of the prizes of political life, which other nations are able to dispense more lavishly, we have felt a certain pride in the fact that our diplomatists stand for the best traditions of American citizenship rather than as the representatives of a caste. The example of Franklin is still a living one. Diplomacy, moreover, is no esoteric mystery, and the qualities of shrewdness and balance apparent in our business and political intercourse are essential to the skillful negotiator. There is no reason why any administration should restrict the selection of its ambassadors to the exclusive choice of candidates appointed thirty or forty years previously, as is the case in certain continental services. There is especially no likelihood of any American government so doing. A rapidity of action and success is still manifest in our public life. We have slight respect for the slow gradations which lead in older nations to positions of dignity. In examining our diplomacy as it now is, these elements of actuality have to be considered. The problem is not to devise an ideal service in an ideal state, but to increase the efficiency of existing methods and adapt them, where necessary, to modern requirements.

The former idea of utilizing the foreign service as part of the spoils system sufficed, however inadequately, for our requirements so long as external questions were of simple order. Even then certain elements of permanence and continuance of policy were found to be necessary, and both the Department of State and several of our missions abroad contained men whose presence outlasted any administration. It seems likely that this tendency will increase in the future. No general can win a battle without lieutenants, and the advantages of a skilled rank and file in diplomacy, as in other public services, has become more widely appreciated. Recent efforts in this direction have certainly given considerable impetus to a movement which must commend itself to all intelligent observers.

The future success of our foreign policy will undoubtedly depend in great measure upon the skill of our diplomacy. The welfare of the nation at large is indeed far more intimately bound thereto than may be commonly believed. An idea has been widely prevalent that with the increase of rapid means of communication and the diffusion of news through the press the importance of diplomats was on the wane. Ambassadors were pictured as clerks at the end of telegraph wires. Had diplomacy been unable to renovate its eighteenth-century garb of court intrigue, this might have been true. But the proof of its utility is that it has conformed itself to modern requirements. It has become economic where economic questions were at issue. It has arranged customs schedules; it has framed discriminating tariffs and forged the weapons for commercial warfare. It has served the ends of finance and industry. The preservation of peace and the diplomatic preparation for war are to-day but its occasional concern. It is the will of the sovereign people, no longer the whim of kings, that determines the graver questions which now preoccupy it. Herein diplomatists can act only as intermediaries, with no power save to register decisions or transmit information. The real scope of diplomacy is both narrower and deeper, — narrower in effecting the settlement of unimportant current questions that are daily met with in international relations; deeper in contributing to lay the broad foundations for a nation's future action by aiding to form its opinion in foreign policy. Herein it becomes the instrument of statecraft in international relations. Its duty to keep the central government informed of everything of interest abroad should serve future as

well as present. And since popular passions
cannot be causelessly stirred, it is the province of diplomacy to see that such occasion
should never arise without good reason.
Diplomatists act thus as the scouts of nations as well as the negotiators; and any
line of foreign policy which does not take
into view their action is hardly likely to
achieve success. The creation of a diplomacy able to supply the mechanism for the
assertion of our foreign policy thus com-
mends itself as a corollary to our future
position in the world. We have built up a
great navy which now provides the material
reserve upon which to base the means of
enforcing our contentions; but the navy is
incomplete without building up our diplomatic service and making of it a useful force
in the national life.

The improvements which remain to be
effected involve no radical changes alien
alike to our traditions and our habits of
thought. The foundations of reform which
have lately been laid in so many directions

have been inaugurated as well in the foreign services with a view to securing that harmonious coöperation of effort essential to success.

The necessity existing for reform arises from the continuance of certain methods that have survived the conditions for which they were originally intended. While a permanent service is able more easily to renovate itself in conformity with new necessities, a transient one can rarely do more than pass to its successor the methods it has received from its predecessor. The efficiency of to-day only too easily degenerates into the sterility of to-morrow, and the utility of any governmental branch finds itself curtailed because its development has not corresponded with the growth of other national activities. While our diplomacy has hitherto amply sufficed for the disposition of current questions, it has hardly as yet adapted itself to the new conditions which confront us, or exercised its full scope as an instrument in the nation's welfare.

The spirit animating a service is the element most conducive to its efficiency, and its infusion into a body can alone weld the latter into a homogeneous whole capable of high achievements. The problem is how to reconcile the conditions of permanence necessary for this spirit with the peculiar exigencies imposed by our political system. The past has left an unfortunate heritage in the artificial separation not only of kindred branches, but of different divisions of one service. The remembrance of a former and purely political method of recruitment of all officials still causes our diplomatic posts abroad to feel perhaps too isolated from one another, and not as parts of one great system bound together by common action inspired by a common purpose.

The diplomatic service, as has been stated, should be the eyes and ears of the nation in its contact with foreign powers. While journalism has to a certain extent taken its place in the communication of news, even at the present day, especially in the older countries, a diplomatist can reach sources not accessible to the press. Information of national interest is usually, however, of a different order from the current news of the press. Its acquisition and its transmission in the shape of studied reports treating of every phase in the life of a country count among the elements which in foreign diplomatic services make most for their utility. The subsequent diffusion of such reports in the form of confidential prints circulated in the service engenders a healthy rivalry which links the post closer together by keeping them informed with regard to events in other lands and the character of the work done by other missions.

In giving greater attention to junior diplomatic officers the administration has wisely recognized in them the element most essential to permanence in the service. The importance of a body of capable secretaries is felt especially in a service such as ours, where the great posts are usually granted to those who have gained prominence at home. A high degree of efficiency can be secured only by the presence of a permanent element more familiar with diplomatic traditions than could be expected of envoys often fresh from civil life. The art of diplomatic forms is acquired mainly by experience and training, and the value of such knowledge, somewhat alien to our habits of thought, cannot be over-emphasized in view of the undue sensitiveness which characterizes the international relations of the continental powers. The ancient tradition of the "point of honor" has survived in the offense so easily taken, especially by European nations, at any departure from the conventions of diplomacy. An ambassador, in spite of otherwise signal ability, may easily find the efficiency of his mission impaired through having given unintentional offense by some trifling breach of form. In this lies the need for an efficient body of secretaries acquainted with traditions and able properly to embellish the phraseology of an envoy whose early training may not have sufficiently prepared him for the necessary suavity of a diplomatic style.

By far the most serious element prejudicial to the unity of our diplomacy lies, however, in the complete division which separates the diplomatic service from the Department of State. In the army we have adopted the system of interchange between the line and the general staff; but in our foreign and departmental services, the methods of recruitment and promotion being entirely different, we have not yet been able to follow the example of other nations who have either fused or assimilated these in grade. In Italy, for instance, by a recent radical reform, all officials at the Ministry in Rome have been given either diplomatic or consular rank, varying with their position. In every European foreign office, moreover, interchange is encouraged between service at home and abroad, thus bringing the personnel of the two branches of one service into close coöperation. With us, although a wise innovation now requires all new diplomatic appointees to undergo a brief period of instruction in the department, the subsequent separation is complete. While the civil-service regulations protecting departmental officials render later assimilation difficult, means could probably be found to obviate this impediment and bring about a closer fusion than now exists, to the advantage of both services. Reform within the diplomatic service can only go hand in hand with reform in the department, and either is well-nigh useless without the other.

With the growing accumulation of work, the limitations of human energy must make themselves felt more and more. When, a century and a quarter ago, John Jay became Secretary of State, his only assistants were two clerks. It is a striking tribute to the devotion to duty of our cabinet officers that even to this day they have retained so great a body of work on their own shoulders. But in spite of the aid of assistant secretaries, actual conditions still seem to impose an unfair tax upon their energy. Amid the rapidly increasing volume of foreign affairs, a body of specialists with diplomatic training would permit the Secretary of State and his immediate assistants to give greater attention to the more important questions, permitting matters of routine and special knowledge to be treated by competent experts. Of late this necessity has impressed itself on nearly all the European foreign offices, which have been reorganized with a view to enlarging the responsibilities of juniors and the specialization of bureaus along political-geographical lines. Where formerly the entire labor devolved on the ministers and under-secretaries, who utilized their assistants in a purely clerical capacity, this order of work has been reversed, and the latter are now given opportunities for proving their worth.

The great advantage in any specialization of bureaus is that it creates a body of experts with detailed knowledge of the affairs of foreign countries. The result has been to obtain a certain standard of action, a certain norm of method, and coördination of parts, which in the conduct of affairs of state takes the place of genius. Ministers of foreign affairs abroad are not dependent on clerks alone to second or to inform them, but can rely on the technical advice of skilled officials possessing expert and usually personal acquaintance with the nations whose affairs they are specially called upon to handle. In Europe the foreign offices are recruited in the same manner as the diplomatic services. Their staff rises to, and interchanges with, similar grades in diplomacy. Their bureaus are presided over by ministers and ambassadors. Their traditions are inspired by centuries of precedent. It is obvious that a weight of moral authority would therefore be attached to the recommendations of the chief subordinate officers which no politically constituted cabinet would override without good cause. Our own State Department, through no fault of its own, can hardly as yet aspire

to the same authority in its recommendations to Congress. Cognate to this there
arises a more important question. It has
often been remarked that we may demand
of foreign states that they live up to treaty
obligations which we ourselves are unable
to enforce. Our mixed order of government
contains unquestionably an element of
weakness in the occasional clash between
federal and state power. The equity of our
contentions abroad can at any time be
undermined by the inability of the government to exercise its authority over sovereign
states. This problem, which only lately
assumed a pressing form, is likely to be
increasingly encountered with the growth of
our foreign intercourse. Among the reasons
which hitherto have militated against any
surrender by the states of their sovereign
rights has been a constitutional unwilling-
ness to see the executive power increased.
The eighteenth-century conception at the
basis of our Constitution looked to a balance
of the different governmental parts some-

what in the nature of a diplomatic equilibrium. New accretions of power by any governmental branch could be viewed only as being at the expense of its other divisions, and contrary to the spirit of the Constitution. Any weakening in the assertion of state rights appeared to signify a corresponding increase in the power of the executive. But this held true only because the administrative branches of the government were directly subservient to the executive and exclusively responsible thereto. Cabinet ministers are still secretaries in practice as in name, and as such theoretically presidential clerks. If the states, therefore, were ever to waive any portion of their sovereign rights in favor of the federal government, yet without unduly augmenting the executive power, it could be done only by increasing the authority of certain departments and removing these as much as possible from the sphere of politics. The formation upon a non-partisan basis of a permanent diplomatic service and State Department would appear to offer an advantageous solution of the problem of equalizing the extension of power accruing to the executive through any abrogation of state rights. The increase of presidential power would be balanced by the fact that any exercise of such authority could be invoked only through the agency of a department semi-independent of the executive, and, save at its head, independent of political change.

The close coöperation not only between the different ramifications of one service, but between the different services of a government, is the condition essential to success, and is especially necessary in an administrative personnel such as our own, composed both of permanent and of temporary officials whose maintenance in office depends on the party in power. The efficiency of our foreign service is conditional as well upon its relations with the other branches of the government. The ability and devotion of officials finds its scope restricted without such coöperation of effort. A line of foreign

policy is frequently adopted in conformity
with the means at a government's disposal.
To assert a pretension impossible to enforce exposes the nation to the danger of
humiliation. A close coöperation between
departments of War, Navy, and State thus
becomes necessary. And while this is already obtained at cabinet meetings, there
are numerous problems that could advan-
tageously be discussed by experts of each
department, who would then be in better
position to advise their respective chiefs.
The general naval board instituted a few
years ago furnishes the type of a similar
advisory council which could to advantage
include representatives of the three departments concerned.

Opportunity for further coöperation
would appear to present itself in the relations between the Departments of State and
Justice. At present, the Secretary of State
is usually apprised through a foreign envoy
at Washington of cases concerning citizens
of his nation, and once such affairs have

been taken up diplomatically, they add to
the labors of the government. If, however,
the federal attorneys throughout the country were instructed to report to the State
Department all cases concerning foreign
subjects, it might frequently be possible to
settle difficulties out of court before they
had attracted public or diplomatic attention and assumed a form complicating their
solution or possibly even embittering international relations.

Our foreign policy is destined by the very
basis of American national existence to be
developed amid conditions differing from
those prevalent elsewhere. In European
states it lies within the power of the executive to frame alliances without having
recourse to parliamentary approval, unless
budgetary considerations be involved. A
British Cabinet is able to negotiate a military treaty with Japan unknown to the British nation, and even republican France can
sign an alliance with Russia the articles of
which still remain a secret. With us the

Senate's necessary ratification, and the consequent publicity in the case of all agreements of a binding nature, entail a radically different procedure. There can be no question that the Senate's action has, in the main, proved beneficial. If its decisions have not always been marked by an appreciation of our future needs, as in rejecting the purchase of St. Thomas, as a rule it has had a very clear comprehension of where lay the nation's interests. Nor is it either likely or desirable that it should divest itself of any of its power in our foreign relations. As a permanent committee, fairly representative of the country at large, it gives the seal of national approval to our policy abroad.

It may be hoped withal that the present tendency to remove certain questions from party considerations will more and more find useful application in foreign affairs. The Monroe Doctrine, which has always been regarded as a non-partisan measure, affords a precedent for this. The European nations, divided internally along party

lines, have yet achieved a stability of policy
in their foreign relations and in questions
of defense. Any other course on our part
would be parading to the world dissensions
where it is most important that none exist. Our external policy should be national
and not partisan. Whatever be its trend,
it should at all times have behind it the
support of the entire country. Of late there
has been a fortunate disappearance of
that lack of sympathy which long existed
between Congress and the Department of
State. The good will of the Senate being
essential, it is only wisdom to take counsel
of its views beforehand and avoid a repetition of so unfortunate an incident as the defeat of the arbitration treaties a few years
ago. Nowhere is close coöperation between
the different branches of government more
important than in diplomatic questions,
where the nation ought to present a united
front. Nowhere is any misunderstanding
so likely to be fatal to our foreign policy or
so disastrous to the efficiency of the ser-

vice. Strength at home permits of strength abroad, and the department's complete harmony with Congress is the primary condition for diplomatic success. It is an unfair tax on any Secretary of State to demand that in addition to attending to administrative duties he be called upon to appear personally before the Senate and House committees on Foreign Relations. This work could be accomplished as well by a congressional secretary charged with explaining details and answering questions of foreign policy. An official who could act as the recognized permanent link between the Senate and House committee, at whose constant disposal he would be, and the Department of State, ready to give to the nation's representatives the information they desired, would be able to avoid misapprehensions and errors on either side, and effect that close coöperation between the executive and legislative branches of the government which is indispensable to the highest success.

A more intimate union of sympathy would further appear desirable between the department and the nation at large. The press has furnished a great medium of communication between the government and the country, and, with the growth of democratic ideas, its importance has been enlarged and its powers strengthened. It therefore becomes of national interest to possess a press ably directed and well informed, which may intelligently influence the masses. Our people have been too little accustomed to judge of foreign affairs. Often they have not fully appreciated the significance of phases in international relations, or again have over-emphasized their importance. The creation of a qualified press bureau in the Department of State, as the recognized channel of communication between the government and the public in all matters of foreign policy, would remove a part of the burden which the reception of newspaper correspondents still imposes upon our public men. The views of the government on questions of foreign policy could be given to the country through the medium of some such channel as those which continental foreign offices possess, and which would allow public opinion to be held in restraint or prepared for any course of action or event. An official whose sole duty would be to inform the press of our national necessities in questions of foreign policy could, without in any way improperly interfering with the independence of its judgment, exert a healthy influence in educating the country by its means to an intelligent appreciation of our international relations.

With our new world-wide responsibilities, the cultivation of a competent public opinion in questions of foreign policy has become an urgent necessity. On the one hand the patriotism of the great majority of the people is too easily led astray by unreasoning enthusiasms which reflect greater credit on the generosity of its feeling than on its mature judgment. On the other there exists the small minority of those who cavil at every manifestation of our influence or authority abroad. Between the two remains to be formed an enlightened and in-intelligent body of opinion competent to judge questions of foreign policy in the same way as it judges questions of interior policy. The press should furnish the vehicle for the diffusion of such opinion. But with a few noteworthy exceptions, it has not yet displayed the same intelligence in considering our foreign interests that it manifests in domestic matters. It is still inclined to treat such questions with a levity or a sensationalism which contrasts unfavorably with the balanced judgment of serious European journals. Keenly avid for news, it has felt less interest in discerning the importance of the information published, or in weighing its consequences below the surface of sensation. It still remains provincial and inadequate to the dignity to which it should properly aspire in its functions.

While the remedy for this condition rests ultimately with the nation, which has not yet realized the importance of foreign questions, the Department of State through the proposed press bureau ought to aim as well to educate the country to a more intelligent appreciation of our interests abroad. In a democracy such as ours, public opinion provides the final sanction against which no government can rule. It becomes of the highest consequence that this opinion be intelligently formed, in order that it may weigh with discernment the needs of the nation in its relations with the world.

CHAPTER VIII

THE FUTURE OF OUR INTERNATIONAL POSITION

Our energy, our resources, and that force of circumstance known as destiny have hitherto contributed to carry us into the forefront of nations. Our rightful place has been won almost without present effort. The Civil War made us a great nation because it proved that we possessed the spirit of national sacrifice. The Spanish War, with its diplomatic significance out of all proportion to its military importance, notified the world that we were a great power. But though possessing the material foundation which entitles us to our new situation, and though filled with a lofty resolution which has hitherto saved the nation's action, even when mistaken, from ever being ignoble, our preparation for the new order of responsibilities before us has been inadequate, and we remain handicapped by a system no longer in conformity with actual requirements. We stand to-day at a transition point where, feeling only the presentiment of our high destiny, we trust rather to chance and the wisdom of the moment than to conscious effort to direct our course.

Every age is as much trustee for the future as it is heir to the past. Foresight is an essential quality of statesmanship, and a government would be remiss in its duty if it failed to take into consideration the needs of later generations. American foreign policy of to-day should be based not only on the expediency of the moment, but on the necessity of maintaining our international position in the manner best calculated to prepare for the future which properly awaits us.

External problems of policy can never be separated from their internal significance, and both the material and moral aspects of

a foreign policy must be either the result or
the cause of similar tendencies within the
nation, and inevitably react on each other.
With the growth of our international relations such elements will become increasingly important. Whatever necessity we
may at present experience for the assertion
of our influence abroad can only augment
in time.   In less than a half century our
population should be one hundred and fifty
millions; were our territory as thickly settled as Germany, it would be nine hundred
millions.

The problem lies in moulding a policy
which will gauge the nation's present and
future requirements in conformity with the
means it has and is likely to possess.   Certain tendencies which must influence our
future course are already apparent. A growing industry will strengthen our interest
in the world's markets, and as we become
more dependent upon our over-sea trade,
closer scrutiny will inevitably be given to
foreign and colonial problems now remote,

and to the navy as a protecting accompaniment of commerce.

The tendency toward increased armaments has received fresh strength from recent developments. Economic reasons will probably one day place a curb upon their further extension, just as economic reasons provide in ultimate analysis the necessity for sea power. But forecasts into the future can, for the present, neglect any schemes of disarmament, and to propose these prematurely would be more likely to defeat their purpose than to aid it. The rapid growth of our fleet in recent years makes it safer to presume that the efforts which have carried us into our present place among naval powers will not soon be discontinued. American diplomacy has every reason to anticipate from it the assistance which armed strength alone is able to confer.

Whatever the future may hold in store for us, we need anticipate as little the birth of an order of events likely to transform us into a world-conquering power as one which will permit the nation to continue its tranquil policy pursued before the Spanish War. Our external problems will diminish only in so far as increased force has made of us a more redoubtable antagonist. While certain of our pretensions are for this reason less likely to encounter resistance than before, consciousness of strength may also lead to difficulties which would once have been avoided. A world position inevitably entails world responsibilities.

Whatever new questions may in time arise, the present problems that confront us are not likely to be dismissed soon. The extension given to the Monroe Doctrine in recent years is certain to make continual demands on our vigilance, even if no stronger measures become necessary. Coupled therewith, the building of the Panama Canal has widened our national interests and placed the countries bordering on the Caribbean in the same relation toward us as was formerly Cuba alone. The necessity to preserve neutral markets has further caused the extended assertion of our influence in the Orient, where we have of late been rudely awakened to the change caused by the rising power of Japan. Everywhere our horizon has been enlarged; everywhere we are called upon to handle new problems both in the light of our own general interests and from the more special point of securing the preservation of the Philippines.

The nation, conscious of its responsibilities and dangers, has in recent years developed its means of defense. The same sentiment must inevitably make toward renovating our diplomacy as the navy's complement in preserving peace and safeguarding over-sea interests. This does not signify the reversal of past traditions. We may preserve their spirit while infusing into them fresh life, enveloping what is vital in a form appropriate to new requirements. The navy would to-day cut a sorry figure if, because the *Monitor* had once proved so serviceable, we had never gone beyond it as a type for our war-ships. Yet in the handling of foreign affairs we have remained "content with a diplomatic service always inadequate and often positively detrimental to our interests." [1] We have not recognized in diplomacy the technique, so to speak, of statesmanship in the nation's foreign relations. Having minimized its rôle as the act of international intercourse, its importance in securing economy of effort has been minimized for us. One cannot draw from a jar more than it contains; and diplomacy has hitherto occupied too minor a part in the national life to have been utilized as the instrument of strength it should be. Its possibilities still remain for us as virgin as were our forests.

Fortunately we can start on our march under unparalleled auspices. Where the nations of the Old World have been obliged hitherto to rely on comparatively slight means, and where their success has depended on a high power of organized efficiency, we are already their equals in ca-

[1] Mr. Olney, *Atlantic Monthly*, March, 1900, p. 289.

pacity for organization, while our resources are well-nigh boundless and our possibilities unlimited. The possession of such national baggage is not without consequence. The fulfillment of certain duties from which we can neither hope nor wish to dissociate ourselves will in the future more and more be impressed upon us. "A nation which is at once the granary, the coal and iron mine, and the cotton field of the world cannot as formerly remain enclosed in its continent, indifferent to what occurs in other parts of the globe. It is too great a parcel of humanity to enjoy the right of isolation. It feels that its power makes demands upon it. Its strength creates a right; this right turns to pretension, and this resolves itself into a duty to pronounce on all questions which the agreement of European powers formerly determined." [1]

While statecraft is in the first instance an enlightened selfishness, and while we are

---

[1] E. Boutmy, *Psychologie du Peuple Américain*, Paris, 1902, p. 337.

paramountly concerned in our own welfare, present and future, in the history of nations, as in the lives of individuals, occasions present themselves when, with little or no risk, the cause of humanity may be advanced. Without indulging in Quixotic dreams of redressing the evils of this world, we may yet look forward to exemplifying in our foreign intercourse certain of the ideals which are at the foundation of the Republic. Our diplomacy must rest primarily on the solid basis of material interest, but it should seek to identify such interest so far as possible with that of humanity. The political legacy bequeathed by our forefathers is not at variance with this ambition. The traditions they have handed down should rather ennoble and spiritualize our aim. No more mischievous illusion exists than the belief that because we are launched as a world power our future course must be one of rapacity, regardless of others' rights. The goal before us has in it nothing that is base, but likewise nothing that may not become

either noble or ignoble. For better or for
worse, a wider scope has been held out. It
rests with us to decide what it shall be.
But our future course affects more than ourselves. Our single action, supreme in one
hemisphere, second to none in the other,
will more than that of any other power
influence the political ethics of the world.

At Gettysburg, almost a half century
ago, Lincoln immortally proclaimed before
a divided nation the American gospel. To-
day, when we are united, his words offer a
reminder that the future should not find us
unworthy of the past. The higher our aim,
the more worthy will it be of those who in
the past served and saved the Republic.

The Riverside Press
CAMBRIDGE . MASSACHUSETTS
U . S . A

Lightning Source UK Ltd.
Milton Keynes UK
UKOW06n2053160817
307421UK00001B/114/P